'If you've ever wished you had enough hours in the day to study how to use yours better, Amantha Imber has done it for you. She has a knack for extracting useful insights from productive people and rigorous research, and her practical, charming book will save you more time than it takes to read.' – Adam Grant, *New York Times* bestselling author of *Think Again* and host of the TED podcast *WorkLife*

'*Time Wise* is a must-read for anyone who feels like there are not enough hours in the day. This book will transform how you approach your workday.' – Greg McKeown, *New York Times* bestselling author of *Effortless* and *Essentialism*

'*Time Wise* is bursting with actionable ideas on how to use your time better. If you want to make the time you spend at work more productive, focused and fruitful, *Time Wise* is a must-read.' – Nir Eyal, author of *Indistractable*

'Lots of people talk about spending time wisely, but Amantha Imber is my favourite: more to the point, more real and a lot more fun. Read this book!' – Jake Knapp, bestselling author of *Sprint* and *Make Time*

'Amantha's laser-like focus on productivity is such a helpful tool.' – Mia Freedman, co-founder, Mamamia Media Company

'An incredibly useful and practical book. Amantha nails the detail and helps you accomplish so much more from every single day. I wish I had read it years ago.' – Sandra Sully, journalist/presenter

'If you value your time, then use it wisely by reading this book. I guarantee it will be time well spent.' – Tim Kendall, former President of Pinterest

'Time is one of our most precious resources. I challenge you to read this book and NOT find practical and useful ways to use yours more wisely.' – Daniel H. Pink, *New York Times* bestselling author of *When*, *Drive* and *To Sell Is Human*

'This is like being invited into the equivalent of a Marvel Avengers "Super-powers Hack" class – lots of fantastic (and oftentimes quirky) tips on ensuring you control your life (vs life controlling you) on your terms, in your way and with a ripple effect on work, play and relationships. *Time Wise* is time well spent.' – Nicole Sparshott, CEO Unilever Australia and New Zealand

'Amantha's expertise and wide range of knowledge she has gathered through her podcast comes to life on these pages. *Time Wise* is full of practical and easy-to-apply tips and tricks from industry leaders that can be applied to any individual trying to live a more productive, happier life as a parent, worker or manager – or all three.' – Laura Mae Martin, Executive Productivity Advisor, Google

TIME WISE

Productivity Secrets of the World's Most Successful People

Amantha Imber

 sourcebooks

Published by Sourcebooks
P.O. Box 4410, Naperville, Illinois 60567-4410
(630) 961-3900
sourcebooks.com

Originally published in Australia and New Zealand by Penguin Random House Australia in 2022
First published in the United Kingdom by Ebury Edge in 2023, an imprint of Ebury Publishing

Cataloging-in-Publication Data is on file with the Library of Congress.

Printed and bound in the United States of America.
POD

'We are not given a short life but we make it short,
and we are not ill-supplied but wasteful of it . . .
Life is long if you know how to use it.'
– Seneca, 'The Shortness of Life'

Contents

How wisely are you using your time?

'The bad news is time flies. The good news is you're the pilot.'
– Michael Altshuler

A few years ago, I came across a meme that was going viral on the internet. It read, 'You have the same number of hours in the day as Beyoncé.'

I immediately thought, 'Hell yeah, I do!' But this was quickly followed by, 'So why haven't I sold more than 100 million records worldwide while parenting twins and championing important feminist causes globally? What on earth have I been doing with my life!?'

I convinced myself it was simply my vocal abilities and the fact that my fertilised egg failed to split in utero that had got in the way of achieving such heights. But it did make me wonder: Do high achievers use their time differently to the rest of us?

Now, unless you are Beyoncé (and let's face it, she's not the target market for this book), you are possibly thinking, 'Maybe they do, but they also have a posse of people to help them deal with an overflowing inbox, serve nutritionally balanced chef-prepared dinners every night, and clean weird stains and smells from their toilet. My life is chaotic and busy! And I have to scrub my own toilet!'

I hear you. As do millions of other people around the world.

Research from the World Health Organization suggests we are working longer than ever before. In 2016, 488 million people globally worked more than 55 hours per week. While you might think that's not so bad – well, it is. Working 55-plus hours a week increases our chance of having a stroke or heart disease by 35 per cent and 17 per cent respectively when compared to working a standard 35 to 40-hour week. Hard work is literally killing us.

And that nasty little virus called COVID didn't help matters.

A survey of nearly 3000 professionals in America found that 70 per cent of those who moved to remote work during the pandemic were now working on weekends. Forty-five percent said they were working more hours since the shift to working from home than they were when they were in the office.

In research that spanned sixty-five countries, software giant Atlassian found that Australians' daily average working hours increased by 32 minutes per day during COVID. And Microsoft's 2021 annual Work Trend Index found that time spent in video meetings has more than doubled thanks to the pandemic, with the average meeting now being 10 minutes longer. And we all know how enthralling and life-enriching video meetings are.

To make matters even worse, we have never been so bombarded with digital messages. According to the Microsoft report, we are sending 45 per cent more chat messages per week compared to pre-pandemic levels, and 42 per cent more chat messages after hours. And we sent 40.6 billion more emails in February 2021 than February 2020. So if you feel as if you are drowning every time you venture into your inbox, you are most definitely not alone.

And just for fun, let's throw virtual school into the mix. That's another full-time nightmare, I mean job, right there. Hopefully that job is well and truly behind us by the time this book hits shelves.

Perhaps it's no surprise that Microsoft reported that 40 per cent of employees around the world were thinking of leaving their employer in 2021.

Work life is tough.

But it doesn't have to be this way.

Back in January 2018, my life was busy. I was running a management consultancy with ambitious growth targets as well as being a mum, a daughter, a friend, a housekeeper and so on. I felt as if I was rushing from one thing to the next, yet somehow I still found hours to scroll through Instagram every week. Priorities, right?

Because it was January, the official month of fresh starts, I was reflecting on the year just passed and what I had achieved. Sure, my business, Inventium, was going well and we were doing great work. But what had I personally done? I had replied to thousands of emails in a very timely manner. I had sent a lot of well-crafted emails, too. I had reacted to requests from my team most hours of every day. I had sat in hundreds of meetings and contributed intelligent-sounding thoughts. But had I done my best work? Not really.

I wanted 2018 to be a bigger and better year. I wanted to transform my working habits, which I felt left much to be desired. I wanted to stop being a slave to my inbox. I wanted to leave the office every day at a reasonable hour to make sure I was always home, without fail, to enjoy evenings with my young daughter. I wanted to end every workday feeling that glorious sense of progress you experience when you get meaningful work done instead of being left thinking 'What did I actually do today?'. I wanted to stop my life disappearing into an Instagram black hole. And I wanted to stop being so damn reactive.

So I started a podcast.

I transformed myself from one of those annoying people who says that they are going to start a podcast, to actually starting one. (So now I am one of those annoying people who drop said podcast into almost any conversation they have.)

The podcast, *How I Work*, was a personal mission. I wanted to understand how the Beyoncés and the Elon Musks of the world used their time differently to the rest of us mere mortals. How did they manage their days, their hours and their minutes so effectively while the rest of us struggle to even hit inbox zero once or twice a year?

High achievers are in high demand. Their inboxes are overflowing, their diaries are packed, their workload all-consuming. Given this huge, unending demand for their time and energy, how on earth do they get things done?

Three years, 150-plus interviews and more than three million downloads later, I can conclude two things.

1. High achievers most definitely do approach their workday differently.
2. Their strategies can improve your productivity and the way you work, whether you are a CEO, a working parent, a university student or anyone trying to keep on top of life.

This book gives access to the answers, secrets and strategies they've each found for making things work. You'll feel as if you have been admitted to an exclusive club as you learn about the best tactics used by the best people in their fields.

I'll show you Wharton Professor Adam Grant's trick for making it easy to get into flow when he starts work every morning. You'll find out how *Broad City* co-creator and co-star Abbi Jacobson uses Imposter Syndrome to her advantage. And how Google's Executive Productivity Advisor, Laura Mae Martin, whips her inbox into shape.

What you won't find in this book are well-worn productivity strategies such as: do your most important task first; set clear goals; and stop checking social media so much. You know all that already. Instead, you'll learn some of the most bizarre, eccentric and often counterintuitive methods to boost your productivity.

You will learn why the ex-President of Pinterest, Tim Kendall, locks his mobile phone in a kSafe for hours at a time. You will hear about how 1800-GOT-JUNK founder and CEO Brian Scudamore asks his assistant to change his email password when he goes away on holiday, so he is forced to take a proper break. You'll discover why newsreader Sandra Sully watches her performance back almost every night.

Hosting *How I Work* is a dream job because I have a fascination with how successful people get it all done.

Ever since I can remember, I've been someone who strives to improve and achieve. Some of my most vivid memories from primary school involve my conscientious and competitive streak – always wanting to be better.

My arch nemesis in primary school was a girl called Bonnie Smart. She lived up to her name. The race to the top of the academic hill was always between Bonnie and me. I felt devastated whenever she scored higher in a maths test than I did. And I felt joyous (and secretly smug) when I pipped her at the post.

My ambition continued past school when I became the youngest person to graduate from Monash University's Doctorate in Organisational Psychology. I had the letters D and R in front of my name by the time I was twenty-four. And did I mention that I was also offered a record deal with a big international label during the first year of my Doctorate because I decided to pursue a career as a singer-songwriter-guitarist on the side? Oh yes I did.

I ended up walking away from the record deal because that's how nerdy I was and still am. I wanted to be a psychologist more desperately than an international rockstar. By the time I hit my late twenties, I started a behavioural science consultancy, Inventium, and with my team, have consulted to some of the world's biggest companies such as Google, Apple, American Express, Deloitte, Disney, Atlassian, Nestlé, Virgin, Visa and even Lego. (Although I have a feeling Lego won't have me back in a hurry after I ran a workshop for a product development team in the 'White Room' at their head office in Billund, Denmark, where I accidentally used permanent marker all over their whiteboard-painted walls.)

I say all this not merely to humble brag (although let's face it, the above paragraph isn't overflowing in humility), but to say that I've always been someone who has my shit together.

But in my mid–late-thirties, my working habits began to deteriorate.

I was running my company through an intense and fast-growth stage, and I was stressed. But when the business most needed me to be at the top of my strategic-thinking game, my work life had become about email and checking my inbox whenever I hit a 'stuck' point (literally every few minutes), being constantly interrupted by pings and dings and team mates, attempting the balancing act of full-time work and being a mum, lacking a feeling of accomplishment at work, *and* forgetting what my own goals even were. And let's not forget mindless scrolling on social media.

So being a fully-fledged psychology nerd, I turned to the academic journals for help. At the same time as I started the *How I Work* podcast, I quickly became obsessed with the science of productivity. I led new product development at Inventium to devise programs to help our clients win the battle against digital distraction and teach their staff how to do deep, focused work. Productivity became my life. And I was constantly experimenting with better ways of working and making work more fulfilling.

And I needed these strategies more than ever. In August 2019, I separated from my husband and father of our daughter, Frankie. Going from seeing my daughter every day to only half that time, settling into my new life as a single parent – not to mention contending with 250-plus days in lockdown and having to completely pivot my business to survive the global pandemic – made life rough.

In the middle of 2020, my CEO and I made the decision to trial the Four-day Week, where staff are paid full-time salaries but are expected to get their work done in just four normal-length workdays. We all had to change the way we work – and we did. Productivity increased by 26 per cent over our six-month experiment, and we made the Four-day Week permanent.

With all the chaos around me and trying to do my full-time job in four days, using my time wisely became my superpower. And from what I have discovered thanks to my guests on *How I Work* and with scientific research to back it up, using your time wisely can easily become your superpower.

The strategies I've learned from the experts I've interviewed on *How I Work* fall broadly into seven categories. This book starts with **Priorities**, where you'll learn how the world's best decide what to aim for, and what to say 'yes' and 'no' to. We will then move onto **Structure** and examine how they proactively organise their days, weeks, months and years. In the section on **Efficiency**, you'll learn a stack of surprising and novel time-saving hacks.

Focus comes next, where you'll see how the people who achieve the most can tune out digital distractions and stay focused on what matters. We will then move into **Reflection**, which shows how my guests have overcome negative self-talk and Imposter Syndrome.

In the section on **Connection**, I'll guide you through how to build solid networks and make meeting new people and forming connections easy. We will finish up looking at **Energy**, and the different strategies my guests have used to bring more joy, gratitude and energy into their working lives.

You can read this book from front to back, or you might want to start with the section that resonates with you strongest – perhaps where you feel you need the most help. You will also find that the sections complement each other – for example, the section on structure requires you think about your priorities (which is covered in the first section, Priorities). And learning how to minimise distractions through the section on focus will help you apply strategies covered across all other sections more effectively.

Pick one or two strategies at a time and commit to experimenting with them for a week or two, until you have habitualised them or want to move onto something new.

Treat this book as your personal guide to dominating your workday the way the world's best do. And as a happy side effect, you might just find that your personal life will benefit too, with more time and energy to dedicate to those you love and the leisure activities you most enjoy.

Okay. Enough chitchat. Let's make you time wise.

PRIORITIES
Determine what matters

You begin your workday with the best of intentions. You have a big presentation to prepare so you open PowerPoint. But within a few minutes of starting, your phone rings. It's your boss. She has an urgent request (although with her, a request to find an appropriately funny and on-topic meme to accompany an all-team email to send sometime next year would be classified as urgent).

Brushing aside negative boss-thoughts, you hang up and turn to her request. But then you think to yourself, 'I'd better do a quick check of my inbox to see if anything genuinely urgent is waiting for me'. Of course it is! Everything in your inbox comes with a false sense of urgency.

You get lost in your inbox but then remember the task your boss has asked you to do. You get back to that. But then your day is interrupted by a Zoom meeting. And then another one. And another. Before you know it, it's 3 pm. And you haven't even made a dent in your big presentation.

If that scenario sounds familiar, you are not alone. Many people run their days reactively. But the crazy thing is: most of us don't even realise it because we never stop to get off the hamster wheel.

It's time to get off that hamster wheel and put a stop to your reactivity. It's time to focus on what really matters.

We will start by looking at the big picture and delve into goal setting and why it doesn't always work. That's right – SMART goals really aren't that smart. We will then spend a bit of time talking about decision-making. You'll learn how to make better decisions, as well as some strategies for making it easier to decide whether to say 'yes' or 'no'.

You'll learn ways to be proactive with where you focus your work efforts. We will cover some simple tips to avoid accepting opportunities you really should decline (even if you're a people-pleaser like me). And we will even cover a method to re-prioritise which meetings you attend to help free you from video-call hell.

Armed with these strategies, you'll be whipping your days and weeks and months into shape in no time. And you can finally give your pet hamster a turn on the wheel.

Goal-setting is broken.
This is how to fix it

To be successful, you need to set goals and work towards them, right? That's what all the self-help gurus say. And most managers would agree. Make sure it's a SMART goal – Specific, Measurable, Achievable, Relevant, and Time-Bound – and then go for it!

Adam Alter, a bestselling author and Professor of Marketing at New York University's Stern School of Business, does not agree. While Alter acknowledges that goals can be helpful signposts and they tell you which direction in which to point yourself, he believes the idea of goal-setting is flawed.

'There's an element of goal-setting that's a little bit broken for me,' Alter explains. 'A goal basically means that until you hit your goal state, you're inherently failing. When you are working towards your goal, you're still failing, failing, failing, until you reach the goal and then you succeed. And the way humans work is that we don't really rest on our laurels, which means we don't really get much joy from achieving a goal.'

Alter describes this as being true for both big and small goals. When we work towards a goal, we are potentially feeling like rubbish because until we reach it, we are in a constant state of failure. And then, when we achieve the goal, we don't feel a lasting sense of accomplishment because what do we do? We immediately set a new goal! So we immediately return to our state of failure. It becomes an iterative process of goal-setting, failure state, success, failure state, success. *Forever.*

While it's useful to know what you want to achieve and the direction you want to take, goal-setting might not actually be the best way to get you there. Alter tries to sit down for a couple of hours every month and think about what direction he is aiming to go in and how he wants to allocate his resources and efforts.

But he doesn't set goals. Instead, he sets systems.

'Instead of saying, for example, "My goal is to write 100,000 words," I reframe it and say, "My system is that every morning for an hour I'm going to write 500 words." And eventually that's going to amount to 100,000 words, but you don't think of it that way. You think of it as a system. This is my system for achieving that end state.'

If the system is an achievable one, the process becomes self-reinforcing because you can achieve it every day and see clear progress. Systems feel much more fulfilling and, as such, Alter says that people feel more motivated when using systems instead of goals. And when our motivation increases, so does the quality of our work.

In the case of writing his next book (Alter has written two *New York Times* bestsellers, *Irresistible* and *Drunk Tank Pink*), he says to himself that he wants to have it written in 24 months, which in a traditional sense could be seen as a goal. Alter then asks himself, 'How many words do I need to have written by when? When am I going to write those words? What's my system going to be for getting there?'

So for Alter, instead of making a very general and generic long-range goal, it becomes a daily activity that he will be doing every day. When he adds that up over time, the system produces the outcome he is aiming for. He literally cannot fail.

Professors Gary Latham and Travor Brown actually investigated the effects of using systems instead of goals with 125 students who had just started their MBA. One group of students was asked to focus on applying strategies to learn more effectively. A second group had to set a goal for what they wanted to achieve in the year ahead, such as the mark they wanted to receive, otherwise known as a distal goal. (I secretly suspect that the MBA students who were in the goal-setting group felt they were the lucky ones – after all, we're talking about MBA students here.)

It turns out they weren't the lucky ones. The researchers found, somewhat ironically, that students who focused on systems for learning more effectively achieved better marks than those who set the goal of achieving high grades.

So why do people perform better when they specify the systems they will apply instead of the marks they want to achieve? Imagine that your strategy or system is to study for two hours every night. As the evening approaches, this strategy feels achievable – after all, you will achieve it in a matter of just two measly hours. This feels feasible, and things that feel attainable also happen to feel motivating and energising. But if your goal is to get a high distinction at the end of semester, it feels far off and is thus a lot less motivating and inspiring.

Put it into action

1. Think about something significant you want to achieve. It might be writing a book, like Alter. It might be to run a marathon. Or to really nail an important presentation at work. Or maybe you want to perfect Adriano Zumbo's croquembouche 'tower of terror' from Australian *MasterChef*'s Season 1 (in which case, please invite me around for dinner when you have achieved this mission).

2. Design a system for how you will get to the end state, ideally a process that you can do every day (or at least on a regular basis to help create a routine). You might set a system to run a certain number of kilometres every day, which gradually increases in the lead up to the marathon. Or you might set aside 30 minutes each morning to rehearse your presentation in the lead up to the big day.

3. Set a mid-point review to ensure that your system is going to get you to the end state within the timeframe you have set.

How mental shortcuts can help us avoid burnout

Wharton Professor and Organisational Psychologist Adam Grant is well known for being a giver. He even wrote the book on it – *Give and Take* – about the benefits of being a giver. But owing to his high profile, Grant receives more requests for his time than he could possibly say 'yes' to. So how does a self-described giver decide when to say 'yes' versus 'no'?

'I used to try to say "yes" to everyone and to everything,' Grant told me. 'But I found that that was impossible as I got busier as my profile was raised outside the ivory tower. I just didn't have enough hours in the day to fulfil all the requests that were coming in.'

Grant ended up coming up with a set of heuristics, which is perhaps not surprising, as we psychologists love a set of heuristics. Heuristics are a set of mental shortcuts that allow us to make decisions and solve problems more efficiently. Grant's heuristics mirrored what he had studied during the research phase for *Give and Take*, when he had looked at the differences between people who were successful or failed givers. Successful givers, he discovered, are productively generous, while failed givers are too selfless and end up getting burnt by the takers whom they have the misfortune of dealing with.

To be productively generous, firstly Grant is thoughtful about who he helps. 'For me, I have a hierarchy of people that I'm trying to support. It's family first, students second, colleagues third, everyone else fourth. At some point, I realised that friends were not in that list and I felt really bad about it. But then I realised my goal in a friendship is not to be helping the person, it's to be a friend.'

Secondly, Grant recognises that he is not going to be equally generous to everyone. He became comfortable with the fact that his colleagues may think that he is less generous than his students do. 'I did not become a professor to try to inspire other professors. I became a professor because I wanted to have an impact on students in the same way that I was really influenced by the great teachers that I'd had. I wanted to try to pay that forward.'

Grant also considers how and when he helps. 'That basically breaks down to saying, "Look, I want to help when I can add unique value and when it does not detract from my energy or my ability to get my own work done",' he explained.

To work this out, Grant reviewed all the different ways he was saying 'yes' to people and tried to figure out which ones he enjoyed and excelled at. 'If people were asking for help in domains where I didn't feel like I had a unique contribution to make, or it was exhausting me, I knew that over time that meant I was going to have less impact.'

Grant ended up homing in on two commonalities. One was knowledge sharing. 'There's almost nothing that brightens my inbox more than somebody reaching out and saying, "I had this question about something related to work psychology. Has anybody ever studied 'fill in the blank'?" I'm like, "Yes, there's a chance to take all that esoteric information that I'm collecting from academic journals and share it with somebody who might be curious about it or who can apply it in some way."'

The other way Grant believed he was uniquely placed to help people was through making mutually beneficial introductions. 'I feel like by virtue of the kind of work that I do, I get to interact with lots of different industries and kinds of people. It's just really fun to connect the dots between two people who could help each other or who could create something really meaningful together.'

'I've tried to focus on those requests and that means that when somebody reaches out and it's not in one of those buckets, I'll let them know that their request is not in my wheelhouse, but if I could be helpful by sharing knowledge or by making an introduction, then I'd be happy to do that.'

Several weeks after I first interviewed Grant on the *How I Work* podcast, I witnessed his process in action. A close collaborator of his from Wharton, Reb Rebele, was about to move to Melbourne, where I am based. Grant sent me a glowing four-page professional reference (yes, four pages! Single spacing!) he had written about Reb, and asked if he could connect us. I wrote back and said please introduce us immediately, if not sooner. And more than two years later, I still catch up with Reb every couple of months and always leave our catch-ups feeling enriched and intellectually stimulated. And also, thankful that Grant practises what he preaches.

Put it into action

1. Reflect on your values and consider the groups or types of people you find it most meaningful to help. It might be friends, family, co-workers, clients, your kids, your partner, your pet chinchilla, or another group entirely. Rank your top four or five most important groups to help you prioritise who you help.
2. Think about what kinds of requests you are uniquely placed to help with, combined with the kind of requests you gain the most joy from fulfilling.
3. Use this newfound awareness to form heuristics (i.e. rules of thumb) to help you make quick and effective decisions as to which requests for your time you decide to say 'yes' to.

Why you need a personal board of directors

It's Friday afternoon and you have a big decision to make over the weekend. You've just been offered a job at a competitor organisation. When you told your boss, she said she will give you a 20 per cent pay increase to stay. Tempting . . . You have until Monday to decide.

You are torn. You feel a sense of loyalty to your boss, which makes the decision even more challenging. You think about talking the decision over with a friend or family member, but it's hard for them to be objective. What you really need right now is a personal board of directors – a concept first introduced to me by Columbia University Professor Rita McGrath.

'When I think about bigger picture issues, I think it's helpful to have a personal board of directors,' Rita explains. 'These are people whose opinion you respect that you can bounce things off.'

McGrath likens the concept to the traditional role of a board of directors. 'When a board is functioning properly, they think about the long-term welfare of the enterprise. They point out when they think something's being overlooked or ommitted. They lend their experience and their wisdom to the endeavours of the organisation. And I think the personal board of directors is much the same.'

For McGrath, her board are people she can reach out to for feedback, who might facilitate a connection to someone with a valuable point of view or expertise, and who might have access to resources that she may not have. 'It's a much more intense relationship than a standard networking relationship. What they say really makes a material difference.'

I conjured up images in my mind of McGrath summoning her personal board of directors to gather around a large table once a month for several hours at a time at the top of a fancy high-rise office building while an assistant brings in oat milk lattes. But McGrath assures me this isn't how it works. She typically reaches out to her personal board of directors a couple of times a year and uses them as sounding boards when she has a big decision to make and wants unvarnished feedback.

Unlike a company's board of directors, McGrath has never formalised the relationship. And in fact, her personal board of directors don't even know they are part of McGrath's board. She does acknowledge that this is not always the case. What matters is being deliberate in deciding who these people will be and leaning into them at critical moments in your career.

Put it into action

1. Reflect on the big career decisions that you are typically faced with – or might be faced with – over the coming year (or years). These decisions might be around job changes, career pivots, pursuing a shiny, new project, starting a business, or investing in an emu farm.

2. Identify people who you think could add an insightful and helpful perspective that would be different from your own. Aim for cognitive diversity – people who think differently from you. Look for people who have different experiences and expertise so you can be strategic in who you go to for different types of advice-giving. But perhaps avoid approaching emu farmers, as they may not have your best interests at heart.

3. You can either formalise the relationship by specifying how often you would like to be able to contact them and what sort of time commitment you anticipate. You might even remunerate your board members in some way. Alternatively, you can keep the relationships informal and not even tell them they are on your board.

The critical step most people miss when making decisions

Think about the last time you had a really big decision to make. Maybe it was whether to change jobs. Perhaps it was which school to send your children to. Or maybe it was if you should move in with a partner. Or whether to get divorced and fly to Mars (although I'll assume you're not Jeff Bezos). How did you go about making that decision?

Emily Oster is an Economics Professor at Brown University. She also happens to have parents who are economists, and she is married to one. I secretly imagine that her family get-togethers involve exciting infographic charts and discussions about statistical significance (my idea of heaven, I should add).

Perhaps not surprisingly, Oster has a framework that she uses for making all big decisions in her life. It's called the Four Fs.

The first F is Frame the Question. 'While this step may sound obvious, it's one that people are not particularly good at,' explains Oster. When faced with a decision such as whether to look for another job, Oster says that most people would simply ask the question 'Should I change jobs or not?' But the big problem with this question is that you don't know what the other choices are.

'It's important to frame the question in a way that's a trade-off between two distinct options – as opposed to a trade-off between a) do this concrete thing (e.g. stay in your job) and b) do something else – where the something else is a sort of imaginary thing, such as changing jobs to one that you don't even know what it might entail.'

The second F is for Fact Finding. To make any decision, you need data and information. Oster spends a lot of her time gathering data that will provide her with evidence she can use to steer her towards one of the options she is weighing up.

The third step is the Final Decision, which like Step 1, may also sound obvious (we are talking about a decision-making framework, after all) – but it's one that often gets unnecessarily delayed. And psychologists have found that having unlimited time to make decisions can actually impair, not improve, how happy we are with the outcomes.

'I think we often let big choices percolate and percolate. And we think about them a little here and a little there and in the shower. And we talk to our partner about them.' So to avoid falling into this trap of analysis paralysis and in extreme cases, not actually making the decision, Oster literally books in a meeting time (even if there is only one attendee – herself) to make the decision.

The final F is Follow Up. 'For big decisions, we tend to think about them as "I'm going to make this decision and then that's it". This

decision will be forever. And of course, for some decisions, that's true, but for many of the decisions that we make, it may not be forever. You may have the opportunity to revise that decision at some other time and we don't always take advantage of that.' As such, Oster always schedules a time to review her decisions and reflect on how they are going.

Deliberately reflecting on decisions allows us to course-correct and even abandon ship, as opposed to just sailing forward on autopilot. I personally think of this final stage like a tripwire that jolts me to question past decisions and look for opportunities to improve, iterate or eliminate.

By using Oster's framework, making decisions (especially major ones) can be transformed from a process you might dread or avoid, to one that feels empowering. And let's not forget the major benefit: *better* decisions.

Put it into action

1. When you next have a big decision to make, first, Frame the Question. Make sure you have at least two concrete options to choose between.
2. Do some Fact Finding. Look for data or information that will help you make an informed decision.
3. Make the Final Decision – and set a meeting time with yourself (or anyone else involved in the decision) to make it.
4. Follow Up on your decision. Schedule a time to review and reflect on whether you need to change course from your original decision.

How asking the right questions will lead you to better decisions

Happiness guru and bestselling author Gretchen Rubin loves a pros and cons list. But she started to find that for many decisions, a pros and cons list didn't actually help. This was particularly true when the pros and cons were fairly balanced or when the two options available were so dissimilar it was like comparing apples and oranges. Like deciding whether to get a pet pug or take up yarn bombing as a new hobby (which, despite its name, is a peaceful and artistic hobby. Google it if you have no idea what I'm talking about).

Rubin realised that, often, the difference between making a good and a bad decision is as simple as the questions we ask ourselves to help make the decision. As a result, she developed several questions to serve her in making better decisions.

The first question Rubin asks herself is which option will lead to what she calls the 'bigger life'. This relates to one of her core values: choose the bigger life. Rubin applied this when it came to deciding whether or not to get a pet dog (yarn bombing wasn't in her consideration set).

'For some people, a bigger life would be a life without a dog because they could travel more freely and have more disposable income. But I knew that for my family, the bigger life was to get the dog. And so we got our dog and we love our dog.'

Rubin also asks herself, 'Is this going to make me happier?' 'Anything that deepens relationships or broadens relationships is likely to pay off in terms of happiness. Anything that helps me learn or grow is so important for happiness,' she explains.

A third question Rubin poses comes from advice she received from her father. She asks herself, 'Will I enjoy the process?' 'We can sometimes decide to do something that we really do not want to do at the time. We potentially put up with all this badness for years because we think there is going to be a big payoff.'

In Rubin's case, this involved training to become a lawyer – the profession she was in before she quit to become a full-time writer more than a decade ago. She didn't enjoy practising law, which according to the American Bar Association, makes her a normal human being: apparently 44 per cent of lawyers would not recommend that young people pursue a career in law.

She could have simply put up with her job as a lawyer, knowing she probably would have made partner in several years. Luckily for her millions of readers, she didn't. But Rubin has also observed people trying to write a book in the hope they might write a bestseller, yet they hate the writing process.

'The problem with not enjoying the process is that a lot of times, things don't work out the way we wish they did. We're not in control of *outcomes*. But we can control the *process*.'

Rubin recounted an experience of writing a book called *Forty Ways to Look at JFK*. 'I loved writing that book and it flopped so hard. It didn't reach an audience. But I loved writing that book and, while I'm sad that it didn't find its audience, I don't regret it because I enjoyed the process so much.'

A final question Rubin asks when making decisions is whether it's something she is doing for her fantasy self or her actual self. 'Am I doing this because it's my idea of the kind of person I would like to be? That's a big warning sign for me.'

For example, one of Rubin's values is to 'Be Gretchen', which means embracing who she is at her core rather than pretending to be something she is not. Rubin gives the example of deciding whether or not to buy linen cocktail napkins because they're on sale. And for Rubin – and indeed for Gretchen – linen cocktail napkins are simply not her thing. But then again, are linen cocktail napkins actually anyone's thing?

Put it into action

1. Determine your core values – the things that matter most to you when you think of living a fulfilling life.
2. Frame these values as questions to help guide decision-making. For example, if living a happy life matters to you, borrow Rubin's technique of asking yourself 'Which option will make me happier?'
3. In addition to thinking about values, always ask yourself, 'Will I enjoy the process?' Try to avoid making choices that are only appealing because there might be a big payoff at the end. The disappointment will be far less if you enjoyed the ride, even if you never get to the destination.

A simple trick to making more ethical decisions

When you think of a bank, ethics is probably not the first thing that comes to mind. But former Commonwealth Bank of Australia non-executive director Wendy Stops thinks a lot about ethics. She even has a test for it.

'When you're doing business, it's very easy to get caught up in the dynamics of following a process or a policy or something like that,' explained Stops on my podcast. And when it's time to make a decision, it can be easy to run on autopilot.

When Stops makes decisions, she adopts what the bank calls the 'should we' test – something that personally resonates with her. This involves putting yourself in the position of the customer, their circumstances and their environment. And asking yourself: 'Is this really the right thing for them?'

Stops gives the example of considering a home loan request. 'Even if a customer could technically get through the process and you could give them a tick at the other end, you have to say, "Is it right?"' In other words, while the bank could do it, it's a question of whether the bank *should* do it.

'It sounds a lot easier than it is in practice. Because if you ask the customer, you might get a different view. They might say, "I really want that loan, please give it to me",' Stops explains. But in applying the 'should we' test, she says that the answer might be 'no' because it's clear that the customer will struggle to pay it. The 'should we' test requires people to think beyond the mechanics of the policy or process. Instead, people need to step back, pause and weigh up if it is really the right thing to do.

For me, the 'should we' test is useful to apply not just to customer decisions, but internally, to staff ones. When COVID hit in March 2020, my consultancy, Inventium, was hugely impacted. We went from having a full pipeline of work to having literally every single job cancelled or postponed. We had to retrench four staff. It was heartbreaking for all involved.

While there were legal requirements to fulfil, applying the 'should we' test brought more humanity to the situation. It made me and my CEO think about what else we should do beyond the bare minimum. We spent hours thinking about how to make the process suck just a bit less for everyone involved. We went through all our contacts and called people who might be hiring in the hope they would have work for our four talented team members. Back when virtual gatherings were not really a thing, we had a long deliberation about whether to do a virtual team farewell gathering. (We ended up deciding that one-on-one conversations would feel more meaningful.) And while retrenchment will never be a joyous occasion, I'd like to think that we made it slightly more bearable for those four team members through our reframing of the situation and the action we took.

Put it into action

1. The next time you need to make a decision about a customer, staff member or any other fellow human being, avoid unthinkingly following processes and policies. Though there will be many times where you could move forward with a decision because it's simply following the rules, resist the temptation to do so blindly. Instead, take a step back and ask yourself 'should we' do it.
2. If the answer is 'no', ask yourself what you should do instead.

Have you overcommitted yourself? You need the Iceberg Yes

A couple of years ago, I was asked to sit on the committee to review the MBA program of a prestigious Australian business school. I asked some vague questions about how much time would be required, but really, I was always going to say 'yes'. Not only do I feel passionately about helping university students thrive in the business world, but Inventium had interviewed many MBA students from this university to fill consulting roles. As a result, I had some strong views on how this particular MBA program could help better prepare graduates for the real world.

So I accepted the invitation. But after my first gruelling four-hour evening meeting in a dark, grey and windowless university meeting room, I immediately regretted my decision.

Co-founder and general partner at seed venture capital firm Character, bestselling author of *Sprint* and *Make Time*, and former design partner at Google Ventures, John Zeratsky, refers to my problem as the Iceberg Yes. 'When we are deciding whether to do something – a project, a job, a volunteer role, and so on – we tend to focus on the visible and exciting part. In other words, we focus on the glimmering peak of the iceberg that sits above the water,' Zeratsky explains.

However, he points out that the majority of the time commitment (i.e. the bulk of the iceberg) floats hidden below the surface. And unfortunately, we can't access the shiny and exciting part without doing everything else, such as four-hour-long evening meetings in a stuffy university meeting room.

Having said 'yes' to lots of seemingly exciting opportunities that came with many hidden hours of arduous and time-consuming work, Zeratsky changed his decision-making process. Now, when people request his time or offer him opportunities, he thinks about the whole iceberg, not just what sits above the surface. Zeratsky reflects on all the work that is involved in getting to the exciting part, instead of just thinking about the tip. He also considers how much time it would take out of his work schedule.

'For example, when I agree to a speaking gig, I also schedule the time to prepare for that gig. It makes it harder to say "yes", but that's actually a good thing.'

Zeratsky points out that the reverse comes with its own benefits – that is, the feeling he gets when he says 'no'. 'When I say "no", I think about the full iceberg I'm saying "no" to, not just the single event or meeting or the idea of the role. I get to savour the feeling of all the work I won't have to do.'

What Zeratsky's method overcomes is a psychological bias called the planning fallacy. Research led by Professor Justin Kruger from New York University's Stern School of Business revealed that people consistently underestimated how much time they need to complete a task. And people weren't just a tiny bit off in their estimates – they were off in a major way. One of Kruger's studies found that a task

people believed they could complete in three weeks actually demanded a whole month. Likewise, a task people expected to take eight days would actually take fourteen – more than 50 per cent longer than they had estimated.

However, Kruger discovered that when people were asked to think about all the facets of the task, the bias reduced. So by applying the Iceberg Yes to your decision-making process and unpacking all the activities that a project comprises, you'll more accurately estimate the time required and have the information to make an informed call on accepting an offer.

As for me, I ended up stepping down from the MBA review committee after many hours of very long meetings. Had I thought about the whole iceberg upfront and acknowledged my hatred of multi-hour-long meetings, my initial decision most definitely would have been a different one.

Put it into action

1. When you are next asked to dedicate time to something or presented with an opportunity, think about all the time and potentially hard work that is required to get to the shiny 'tip of the iceberg'. And if you are unsure of the time commitment and exact responsibilities, make sure you ask!
2. Map out all the tasks required and approximately how long each one will take.
3. After reviewing everything required that sits underneath the iceberg's peak, you are now in a far better position to decide whether to say 'yes' to the opportunity.

Never regret a decision again with this simple question

When someone asks us to do something on a day that is far-off in the future, it can be easy to say 'yes'. I know that for myself, when I am asked to do something such as speak at an event that is four or five months away, I think to myself, 'That sounds fun! And my diary is practically empty! So, yes!' But what inevitably happens is when the event rolls around, I start to regret my decision because my diary is, surprise surprise, not looking so empty anymore.

If you are a people-pleaser like me and struggle to say 'no', the easiest thing to do when someone asks you to do something in the distant future is to say 'yes'. Sigmund Freud famously referred to this drive as the Pleasure Principle – our tendency as humans to seek pleasure and avoid pain. But unfortunately, while this tendency results in short-term pleasure (the ability to say 'yes' and please the person asking us), it can lead to long-term pain (having to honour a commitment you possibly didn't want to do).

Athlete and all-round motivational guru Turia Pitt frequently found herself falling into this trap. She is regularly asked to give speeches, but often, they are scheduled for far off into the future. 'I think to myself, "Oh, it's in six months' time, whatever, it'll be fine." And then when the speech is looming, I'm like, "Oh my gosh, why did I say 'yes'?" When I say "yes" to too many things, I end up being really shitty and resentful and not having any time leftover to go for a run or to spend with my family and things like that.'

Instead of falling into the trap of underestimating how busy the future will be and avoiding the short-term pain of saying no, Pitt now asks herself a question before giving an answer. 'I ask myself, "If this opportunity or event was happening next Tuesday, how would I feel about it? Would I be like, Yes! I cannot wait for that to happen, or would I be dreading it?"'

By pausing to ask this question, Pitt is overcoming a key flaw in how humans are naturally wired to make decisions: activities in the distant future seem far more appealing and exciting than those in the more immediate future.

In a study published in the *Journal of Personality and Social Psychology*, participants had to evaluate various activities and plans, such as a government policy or a creative approach to administering exams. The researchers found that activities that were scheduled in the distant future were perceived more favourably compared to those in the immediate future.

When events and plans are set to take place imminently, we are more in tune with potential complications, whereas we are less discerning when things are in the far-off future.

By asking herself the Next Tuesday question, Pitt can focus on how she genuinely feels about the opportunity being presented. By using the Next Tuesday rule, we avoid saying 'yes' to opportunities indiscriminately (and underestimating potential downsides), which can be all too easy if you're the kind of generous go-getter like Pitt.

Put it into action

1. When you are next asked to do something or presented with an opportunity that will happen in the distant future, resist the urge to give an immediate answer.
2. Instead, ask yourself the question: 'If this opportunity were happening next Tuesday, how would I be feeling about it?
3. If the answer is anything less than 'totally pumped!', say 'no'. While saying 'no' can feel challenging, you'll avoid feeling pain and resentment about the opportunity in the long-term.

How to decide which meetings you should attend

'I wish I had more meetings to attend,' said no-one ever. For the average worker, meetings are the bane of their existence and the reason why people often find themselves doing their actual job well into the evening, because this is the only time it's possible to escape meeting purgatory.

Research has consistently found that satisfaction with meetings predicts how satisfied we are with our jobs overall. One study found that more than 15 per cent of our job satisfaction is based on our satisfaction with the meetings we attend. And other studies have found that meeting satisfaction is the *single biggest* predictor of job satisfaction. So it really is mission critical that time dedicated to meetings is time well spent. And one of the most effective things we can do is to prioritise which meetings we agree to attend.

Professor Scott Sonenshein has thought a lot about meetings. He has also sat in a lot of them. When Sonenshein first joined the School of Business at Rice University in Houston, Texas, about fifteen years ago, he remembers attending his very first faculty meeting.

'What really struck me is how much time we just sat there and how we would fill up time,' Sonenshein recalled. 'There was an hour and a half scheduled, and no matter how big or small the issues were that we were supposed to talk about, we always at least filled up that hour and a half.'

Sadly, he had to endure nine of these meetings every year, and despite the lack of value they added, they remained on the calendar by default. When a new dean joined a year later, he questioned if this recurring meeting really needed to be there. And in the blink of an eye, those nine meetings were reduced to three per year. The other six were sorely missed. Kidding. Of course they weren't.

Research suggests meetings often happen out of habit as opposed to need. And as a result, people complain they have too many meetings in their diary and that they are a waste of time. To address this time wastage, Sonenshein designed a process to help everyone clean up their meetings. He recommends going through your diary and, for every meeting, asking three questions:

1. Is this meeting required for my job?
2. Does it bring me closer to my ideal work life?
3. Does it bring me joy?

If a meeting doesn't fulfil at least one of the above criteria, you are better off not to attend as it will be a poor use of your time.

Sonenshein acknowledges that this is easier said than done. 'People have meeting FOMO. If we don't have a seat at the table, it means that we're not worthwhile, or we're going to miss out on an important decision. And some people mistakenly believe that the person who attends the most meetings is working the hardest.'

We need to let go of meeting FOMO and of equating our status with meeting attendance. Meetings should purely be a way of getting work done and making progress. Meetings are simply not worth going to if you're not getting work done in them. And checking your emails surreptitiously while a meeting is happening doesn't count as 'work'.

Put it into action

1. Go through your calendar and write down all the meetings you have attended in the last two weeks. You could also do this activity looking ahead to the next two weeks' worth of meetings. For each meeting, ask yourself the following questions:

a. Was it required for my job? For example, did it give you information that you couldn't have learned from reading something? Did it help solve a problem? Did it lead to a critical decision?

b. Did it help move me closer to my ideal work life? For example, did you learn something that would help advance your career or learning?

c. Did it bring me joy? For example, did it make you feel more connected to co-workers? Was it fun?

2. Eliminate all meetings that don't meet at least one of the above criteria to help prioritise your time effectively. If you are the organiser, delete these meetings in your calendar. Don't forget to explain why you are deleting them. And if you're a participant, speak to the organiser about your purpose in the meetings. Make any necessary adjustments as required. And if you still feel the meeting isn't relevant to you, then politely excuse yourself.

3. Download a simple one-page template of this strategy at amantha.com/timewise

Why you need to strive for work-life *im*balance

At some stage in your career (or perhaps almost every day), you have probably felt that work–life balance was lacking from your life. Perhaps you've heard leaders in your organisation talk about strategies they are putting in place to help people achieve better balance. And maybe you've read articles giving you advice for how to achieve that elusive, perfectly balanced life. Whatever that looks like.

For global employee engagement expert Marcus Buckingham, the idea of finding work–life balance is flawed. 'The categories of work–life balance are wrong,' Buckingham argues. 'Work is part of life, just like family is part of life, and community is part of life. And it's not like life is good and work is bad, and you have to balance out the bad of work with the good of life. Those are false categories. What we have in life, whether it's work or family or community, are a lot of different aspects and some of them we lean into and some of them we are repelled by.'

Buckingham proposes that instead of trying to balance work and life, we need to look at what we love doing and what we loathe doing. And we need to strive for imbalance. That's right – we need to do the exact opposite of what so-called experts say we need to strive for. 'We should be desperately and always unbalancing our life towards more activities that we love and that invigorate us, and away from those we loathe.'

You may be thinking this relates to the well-trodden career advice: 'Do what you love'. But for Buckingham, this is very unhelpful advice.

'"Find love in what you do" is much more helpful,' Buckingham explains. 'We know from Mayo Clinic data that if you're a doctor and less than 20 per cent of your work activities are things that you love, with each percentage point below 20 per cent, there's a commensurate one percentage point increase in burnout risk.'

In other words, there is a strong negative relationship between doing things that you love, and burnout. If you do fewer activities that you love, your risk of burning out goes up.

Conversely, Buckingham says that spending a lot more than 20 per cent of your work time doing activities that you love doesn't lead to an equivalent decrease in burnout risk. 'If you're spending 25 per cent, 35 per cent, or even 40 per cent of your time at work doing things that you love, you don't get a commensurate increase in resilience and a decrease in burnout. So it seems as though a little love goes a long way.'

Buckingham describes this 20 per cent as Red Thread activities. They are the tasks that lift you up, invigorate you – tasks you happily lean into. 'Time goes by faster when you're doing them and you look forward to them. And it's important to pay attention to the particular activities that we really love.'

To try to create imbalance in his own life and better prioritise his time, every single Friday Buckingham reflects on the week just gone and asks himself what activities he loved doing and what he loathed. He then tries to consciously design the week ahead to incorporate more of those he loves, and less of those he loathes.

Put it into action

1. At the beginning or end of every week, reflect on the week just gone and list all the activities that you loved doing and all the things you loathed doing.
2. For the activities you loved doing, make a plan for how you could do a little bit more of them.
3. For the activities you loathed doing, see if you can reduce them by doing one of four things Buckingham suggests:

- Could you stop doing them altogether? It's possible no-one will even notice if you stop putting together that monthly report that people pretend to read, but no-one actually does.
- Could you team up with someone who loves doing the thing you loathe and ask them to take it on? You might even be able to help them by doing something that they loathe but you love.
- Could you use one of your strengths to mitigate the thing that you loathe? For example, Buckingham hates mingling but he loves interviewing. So he views events and parties as an opportunity to interview people, as opposed to mingle.
- Could you change your perspective and reframe how you view the loathed activity? For example, if you have to fire someone and are dreading having to do it, could you reframe this as an opportunity to release them from a job that they are not thriving in and free them up to find something they will love and excel in?

How to be time wise on Friday afternoons

It's easy to get to Monday morning and spend a good chunk of time trying to recall what on earth you were working on the previous week. Once you've finally remembered what you are employed to do and attempted to avoid drowning in your inbox, an hour or more has quite possibly passed. You now feel overwhelmed with the crazy week that lies ahead. Or maybe you just feel guilty that you've just wasted time getting on top of things that slipped from your mind thanks to a temporary case of work amnesia. It can feel like a Monday-morning mess.

Laura Vanderkam is a world-renowned expert on time management. She has written several critically-acclaimed books on the subject. Vanderkam avoids the Monday-morning mess by setting aside 20 minutes every Friday afternoon to plan the upcoming week.

'I find that it's really hard to start anything new on Friday afternoons, but I'm willing to think about what Future Me should be doing,' explains Vanderkam. 'Taking a few minutes to plan turns what might be wasted time into some of my most productive minutes of the week.'

Vanderkam reviews the week ahead and makes a short, three-category priority list: Career, Relationships and Self. Forcing herself to use all three categories helps her avoid falling into the trap of being overly work-focused – a trap many high-achievers and Type A personalities fall into. And if the idea of setting priorities for your Self sounds absurd, that's possibly a clue that you're a Type A, like me.

'Sometimes, I already have things on the calendar that I'd like to accomplish in these buckets. Sometimes I need to actively schedule it in. In any case, I list these and figure out roughly when they can go in my calendar.'

Vanderkam then organises any logistics and does a calendar triage, whereby she removes anything that shouldn't be there. And when Monday morning comes around, kicking off the week becomes effortless. No Monday-morning mess for Vanderkam.

At a micro level, when she finishes work for the day, she takes a few minutes to write down the following day's to-do list based on what's in the calendar and on her weekly priority list. She keeps this list short – it might contain only five items. 'I would never do a long list of, say, twenty-five items. There's no point in putting something on a to-do list and then not doing it, right? It's just as "not done" as if it never went on the list. Only now I feel bad, too.' But if you are someone who happens to get peace of mind from a long to-do list, aim to keep that one separate from your daily list that only contains your most important tasks.

Put it into action

1. Book a 20-minute meeting with yourself every Friday afternoon. Three or four o'clock tends to work for many people given this is essentially 'dead time'. (I don't know anyone who does their best work late in the day on a Friday.)

2. Draw up three columns on a sheet of paper with the following headings: Career (anything to do with work), Relationships (anything to do with connecting with the most important people in your life), Self (anything to do with looking after yourself).

3. For each category, write down at least one important thing you want to achieve in the following week. For Career, there might be an important project you want to make progress on. For Relationships, you might try to organise a catch-up with a friend you haven't seen in a while, or plan something special to do with your family. And for Self, you might

set aside time to read a few chapters of a great book, get a massage, or do a couple of sessions at the gym. (Note: to make this process even easier, you could refer to your Closed list if you follow Oliver Burkeman's prioritisation strategy on page 46).

4. Open up your calendar and timebox (that is, book a meeting with yourself, also known as timeblocking) when you are going to make these activities happen. If you are struggling to find time, look at what can be either removed or rescheduled in your calendar in the upcoming week.

5. Take a few minutes at the end of every day to review your weekly priority list and create a short to-do list (ideally no more than five items) as to what you want to accomplish the following day.

A daily ritual to help you see the bigger picture

For over a decade, Gary Mehigan was one of the three judges that graced Australian television screens on *MasterChef*, giving feedback on delicious dishes that people like me had a snowflake's chance in hell of replicating at home. But long before Mehigan became a household name, he was in the business of running restaurants.

In his first year of running a restaurant, he nearly lost everything. He physically couldn't have worked any more hours – yet working such crazy hours wasn't translating into more money coming through the door. He was putting out fires all day and had lost sight of the big picture. So Mehigan and his business partners decided to engage a business coach to help turn things around.

'The best thing that the coach did was give me a simple page to fill out at the end of every day,' recalls Mehigan. 'It was a little bit of self-analysis and a quick reset for the following day. It meant at the end of the night, I would go home, have a cup of tea, and gather my thoughts.'

The first few questions required Mehigan to reflect on his day. What had the day been like? How was he perceived by other staff members? Was there anything he reacted really well or really poorly to? 'The first few questions were very quick to answer and felt like writing in a diary,' Mehigan explains.

The next question – what needs to be achieved tomorrow? – switched his mind to the following day and made him consider what he had to accomplish and how to make a difference. 'I would try to think about what's the one thing I can do above and beyond what I do every single day that's going to make a difference.'

The final questions asked him to reflect on staff and consider who he could spend more time with, and who he could teach. These questions forced him to think about who he had neglected in the business or who he hadn't spent much time with in recent weeks.

The following morning, Mehigan would have a quick read of his one-page summary and begin his day with direction.

He found that the hardest thing about religiously completing the one-pager was that it exposed his weaknesses. For example, he would often reflect that he hadn't spent enough time with certain staff members. When he found himself writing down the same names again and again, it would be a trigger to talk to them the next day.

For instance, he used to walk into his restaurant every day and see Barbara, his barista. One morning, thanks to the one-pager, he asked her 'How many coffees do you think you're going to sell today?' Mehigan admits these were big questions for Barbara, since she was more focused on making the coffee as opposed to sales. But once he started talking to her about these goals, her behaviour started to change and Barbara's goals started to align with Mehigan's.

'When I got lazy and didn't do it, I found that my performance and direction dropped off, and other people's performance and direction dropped off too.'

While it would only take Mehigan around ten minutes at the end of the day to complete the one-pager, he found it invaluable. And as a result, it's become one of the first tools he passes on to any new manager to help them spend their time more wisely.

Put it into action

1. Make time at the end of every day to reflect and refocus. It should only take you about ten minutes.
2. Think about the questions that would serve you best. You might consider having three categories, like Mehigan.

The first category asks you to reflect on your day:
- What was the day like?
- How was I perceived by other staff members?
- Was there anything I reacted to really well or really poorly?

The second category focuses you on the following day:
- What do I need to achieve tomorrow?
- What is one thing I can do tomorrow – above and beyond what I normally do – that will make a difference?

The third category focuses on people:
- Who am I going to talk to / spend time with?
- Who am I going to teach?

3. The following morning, have a quick read of your summary and get started with your day.
4. Repeat daily.

Get more done with a Might-Do list

For several years, I have kept two to-do lists for work (that's how much I love them – one just wasn't enough). One of my lists contains tasks that require deep, focused work and demand a decent chunk of time. The other list is for quicker and easier tasks, things that don't require much brainpower. But what happens to this list is that because I tend to avoid administrative work, it builds up (as does my guilt for not working my way through this list every day).

John Zeratsky, who used to work at Google Ventures and co-wrote the bestselling books *Sprint* and *Make Time*, used to-do lists for much of his career. He even designed a couple of custom to-do list apps. He would put things on his to-do list and then work directly off it – because if something was on the list, it must be important. Over time, he realised he was becoming myopically focused on the tiny items on his to-do list, instead of focusing on the big-picture items that matter.

So he thought about a new way of conceptualising his to-do list.

'When it comes to little things I have to do, I keep track of them on a Might-Do list,' Zeratsky told me. 'Instead of a to-do list, it's a list of things that I *might* do. It might sound like a silly distinction but for me it's an important perspective shift, because when you put something on a to-do list, you are both making a record of it and committing your future self to doing it.'

The fact that items on a Might-Do list seem optional is one of the keys to the effectiveness of this strategy. As humans, we prefer activities that we choose to do instead of things we feel forced to do. In a study published in the *Personality and Social Psychology Bulletin*, people were asked to imagine visiting a supermarket with a friend.

Participants were paired with a friend and then told to purchase six products for another person. They were told that three of the objects could be self-chosen (a mug, a chocolate and a pen) and that their friend would pick the other three objects: a small figurine, candy and a ruler (which in my mind makes them sound like a small child). Two minutes later, participants completed a task that subtly assessed how they felt about these six objects. Researchers found that people were significantly more likely to value the objects they chose over the objects their friend chose, due to having the freedom of choice.

The other benefit Zeratsky found in the Might-Do list is that it removed the daily pressure of tending to the little things. He now creates administrative time blocks on some days where he will work through his Might-Do list.

'Every once in a while, when I feel the little stuff piling up, I'll do a full admin day,' explains Zeratsky. And instead of dreading it, he started to enjoy these days because it meant that the smaller, less impactful, tasks that were previously creeping into every single day could be conquered all in one go.

Put it into action

1. Create a to-do list called the Might-Do list.
2. Use this list to record all non-urgent administrative tasks that have a habit of distracting you from your most important tasks. Because the list is called Might-Do, you can relish the choice of doing, or not doing, these tasks.
3. When you observe entries on the Might-Do list building up, simply block out some time – it might be a few hours or even a whole day – to batch process them and work through them in one sitting.

Why you need to put a limit on your to-do list

Perhaps you've tidied up your to-do list with John Zeratsky's Might-Do list approach (see page 44). If you haven't, your to-do list might still be overflowing with items. Perhaps you are imagining the state of your current to-do list and feeling overwhelmed by all its entries? And if you now plan to put this book down after feeling to-do list guilt (you should be working, not reading!), it can often be hard to know where on earth to start.

Guardian columnist and bestselling author Oliver Burkeman used to frequently experience 'to-do list overwhelm'. He would look at everything he wanted to get done and wonder how on earth he was going to accomplish it all. But then he discovered Jim Benson's Personal Kanban philosophy.

'This has been one of the life-changing ideas that I've encountered in the last few years,' recounts Burkeman. 'The basic idea is that you set a really low ceiling on the number of tasks you are going to allow to be actively on your plate at any one point.'

How Burkeman implements this in practice is he has two to-do lists. One list is his Open list, which is endless. 'It's got all the 300 things you have said you'll do or want to do or are thinking about doing.'

Burkemen's Open list concept is not dissimilar to Zeratsky's Might-Do list, but what makes the strategy different is the addition of Burkeman's second list: his Closed list.

'Let's just say the Closed list has five slots on it. You move five things from the Open list to the Closed list. And the rule is: no more things move from the Open list to the Closed list until there's a new slot freed up by one of them being completed. So then you work on one of those five tasks. When it's finished, you cross it out and you can add a new one to your Closed list because it now only has four items on it.'

Now let's get back to the current state of your to-do list. If you currently have a million things, or let's say even ten, on your list, you are potentially hopping between them all and using your time in an unplanned way. And whenever one project gets a bit uncomfortable or intimidating, you can bounce off to another one. Sadly, the result is that you never make meaningful progress on any of them. And that's the case if you're a CEO, a busy parent or a student.

Burkeman found this approach had an even bigger impact than he imagined it would. 'It brings you right into contact with your finitude or your limitations, because it's actually always the case that you can only be working on a few things at the one time. But what this approach does is it makes you conscious of it and helps you make a wise decision about which ones.' Indeed, when the word *priority* came into the English language in the 1400s, it was singular – meaning we could (and should) only have one priority at a time. It was only in the 1900s that the plural form started to be used, referring to priori*ties*, which is actually illogical as, technically speaking, we cannot have multiple things that all come first.

Put it into action

1. Create two to-do lists: an Open list and a Closed list.
2. Move all your current tasks to your Open list.
3. Decide how many active tasks you would like to have on your Closed list. Burkeman recommends between three and five.
4. Pick the most important tasks from your Open list and move them to your Closed list to fill up all available slots.
5. Go to your Closed list when you are deciding what work to focus on.

6. When you tick off a task from your Closed list, pick a new item from your Open list to move to your Closed list.

7. Finally, when new things emerge for you to work on, put them on your Open list. And remember, they can only move to your Closed list when space is freed up.

PRIORITIES
A summary

Set systems, not goals
Think about something big you want to achieve. Design a system for how you will get to that end state, ideally where you can do something every day (or at least on a regular basis to help create a routine).

Create decision-making heuristics
Reflect on your values and consider the groups or types of people you find it most meaningful to assist. In addition, think about what types of requests you are uniquely placed to help with, combined with the types of requests you gain the most joy from fulfilling. Use this newfound awareness to form heuristics to help you make quick and effective decisions as to which requests for your time you say 'yes' to.

Assemble a personal board of directors
Identify people with different experiences and backgrounds who could add an insightful and helpful perspective for the big decisions you make in life. This group will form your personal board of directors. Consult them for their opinions – whether formally or informally – whenever you reach a significant crossroads and are facing a range of options.

The Four Fs decision-making framework
When you next have a big decision to make, first, Frame the Question. Make sure you have at least two concrete options to choose between.

Next, do some Fact Finding. Look for data or information that will help you make an informed decision. Then, set a meeting time with yourself to make the Final Decision. Finally, Follow Up on your decision. Book time in your diary to review and reflect on whether you need to change course from your original decision.

Ask values-based questions to make better decisions

Think about your core values – the things that matter most to you when you think of living a great life. Frame these values as questions to help guide decision-making. For example, if living an altruistic life matters to you, ask yourself, 'Which option will have a more positive impact on others?' On top of thinking about values, always ask yourself, 'Will I enjoy the process?' Avoid making choices that are only appealing because there might be a big pay-off at the end.

Ask 'should we', not 'could we'

While there will be many occasions where you could move forward with a decision because it's simply following the rules, resist the temptation to follow rules blindly. Instead, take a step back and ask yourself if it's something that should be done. If the answer is 'no', consider what you should do instead.

The Iceberg Yes

When presented with an opportunity, map out the total time and potentially hard work that is required to get to the exciting 'tip of the iceberg'. After reviewing everything that sits underneath the iceberg, you will be in a far better position to decide whether to say 'yes' to the opportunity.

The Next Tuesday rule

When you are asked to do something that is happening in the distant future, ask yourself the question: 'If this opportunity were happening next Tuesday, how would I be feeling about it?' If the answer is anything less than excited, say 'no'.

Clean up your meetings

Go through your calendar and flag all the meetings you have attended in the last two weeks. For each meeting, ask yourself the following questions:

1. Was it required for my job?
2. Did it help move me closer to my ideal work life?
3. Did it bring me joy?

Eliminate all meetings that don't meet at least one of the above criteria.

Conduct a weekly Love and Loathe review

At the start or end of every week, reflect on the week just gone and list out all the activities that you loved doing and all the things you loathed. For the activities in the first category, plan how you could do more of them. For the activities that you loathed, reduce them: stop them, delegate them, use a strength to mitigate the effects of having to do them, or reframe how you view the activity that you loathe.

The Three-Category weekly review

Book a 20-minute meeting with yourself every Friday afternoon. Draw up three columns on a sheet of paper with the following headings: Career, Relationships, Self. For each category, write down at least one important thing you want to achieve in the following week. Timebox when you are going to make these activities happen.

Start a daily-reflection ritual

At the end of every day, take 10 minutes to reflect. First, reflect on your day by asking what it was like and how you reacted to things. Second, look ahead to tomorrow. Ask yourself: 'What is one thing I can do tomorrow – above and beyond what I normally do – that will make a difference?' Third, think about other people. Ask yourself who you will spend time with and who you will teach. The following morning, have a quick read of your summary and get started with your day.

The Might-Do list

Create a to-do list called the Might-Do list. Record all non-urgent administrative tasks that have a habit of creeping into your day and distracting you from your most important tasks. Because the list is called Might-Do, you can relish the choice of doing, or not doing, these tasks. When the list starts building up, block out some time to batch process the items.

The Open and Closed lists

Create two to-do lists: an Open list and a Closed list. Move all your current tasks onto your Open list. Set a limit (e.g. three) of how many active tasks you will have on your Closed list. Pick the most important tasks from your Open list and move them to your Closed list to fill up all available slots. When you tick off a task from your Closed list, pick a new item from your Open list to move to your Closed list.

STRUCTURE
Shape your day

It's Monday morning and you log on to your computer, brimming with energy. You have your priorities straight and know exactly what you want to achieve this week. Unfortunately, you make the mistake of taking a sneaky look at your email before getting into your most important task for the day. In an instant, your focus has turned from proactive to reactive.

You are immediately hit with several 'urgent' requests from team-mates and your boss. You tab over to your calendar to look for gaps of time where you can fit this work, but lo and behold, meetings have spread like an aggressive virus in your diary without you even realising. You feel your stress levels rise. Your fantasy of focusing on your most important task is a distant memory.

But don't worry – you're not alone.

When it comes to a standard work week, most of us play defence. Meetings are scheduled in our diaries by co-workers, the emails we receive determine our priorities throughout the day, and everything that people want from us feels urgent. Days feel like an ongoing game of Whac-A-Mole – but not in that 'I'm having fun at a fairground' kind of way.

It's time to take control and move into offence.

This section will help you proactively structure your weeks and your days to optimise how you spend your time. You'll learn the latest science on when to schedule particular types of activities. You'll learn about why you need to book breaks in your diary, rather than just crossing your fingers and hoping you'll have time for one. And you'll get advice on how to end every workday on a high (without the use of drugs).

Why you need to let your chronotype shape your day

Most productivity advice fails to consider a critical factor that underlies its effectiveness: your chronotype. Your chronotype is the natural 24-hour sleep-wake cycle that influences the peaks and troughs of your energy throughout the day.

Around one in ten people are what chronotype researchers refer to as larks. Larks are stereotypical 'morning people'. They happily jump out of bed at or before sunrise without having had to set an alarm. You will recognise larks as those smug members of the 5 am club that you see posting on social media about how much they have achieved before everyone else has dragged their sloth-like bodies towards the first coffee of the day. (At this point, I should confess that I am a lark. I promise not to show off about the fact that I've been writing since 6 am this morning. But, since you asked, I have been.)

Larks are deeply irritating to owls (and let's face it, anyone who is not a lark). Owls sit at the other end of the chronotype continuum. They represent around 20 per cent of the population. As the name suggests, they come to life at night.

Everyone else is a middle bird: they are neither bright-eyed and bushy-tailed in the morning, nor burning the candle well into the night. Middle birds tend to follow

LARKS

MIDDLE BIRDS

the rhythms of a lark, albeit delayed by a couple of hours.

Larks and middle birds experience peak cognitive alertness in the two hours after they are fully awake. They have a post-lunch energy dip and then experience a second wind in the late afternoon. Owls' days follow the reverse pattern.

Now, you might be thinking, 'Isn't this distinction between morning and evening people just an excuse for owls to justify staying up late on a Netflix binge? Or for larks to be sanctimonious members of the 5 am club?' Not at all. It turns out that understanding our chronotype and structuring our work around it makes us a whole lot happier (not to mention a lot more productive) at work. For example, research conducted in Iran with 210 healthcare workers found that larks experienced more enjoyment at work if they worked morning shifts. Likewise, owls received more joy from work if they were rostered on for evening shifts.

When writing his *New York Times* bestselling book *When: The Scientific Secrets of Perfect Timing*, author Dan Pink began digging into this research. On discovering that he was a middle bird, he completely restructured his workday.

'I changed my schedule so that on writing days, I set myself a word count and in the morning I'll say, "Okay, today I have to write 700 words" and I won't bring my phone into the office with me, I will not open up my email, I will not do anything until I hit those 700 words and then I'm free to do other things,' Pink explains.

OWLS

'I use the early to mid-afternoon typically for answering email and filing and scanning things – the kind of stuff that doesn't require a heavy load,' says Pink. 'And then when I come out of the trough at around three or four o'clock in the afternoon, I tend to do interviews or things that don't require me to be locked down and vigilant, but just to be open to possibility, open to ideas, and a little bit more mentally loose.'

As a result of sticking to this schedule, *When* was the only book Pink submitted to his publisher on time.

Put it into action

1. Start the process of restructuring your day by completing the Morningness Eveningness Questionnaire here: amantha.com/timewise

2. Plan your workday based on your chronotype. Use your score from the Morningness/Eveningness questionnaire to help you decide when you should be doing your most focused and deepest work, and when you should be doing less cognitively demanding work.

3. Use these guidelines below to help structure your day:

For larks (definite morning):

Deep work	7–10/11 am
Shallow / Light work	11 am–2 pm
Rebound (for additional deep work)	2–4 pm

For middle birds (moderate morning/evening and intermediate):

Deep work	9 am–12 pm
Shallow / Light work	12 pm–2/3 pm
Rebound (for additional deep work)	3–5 pm

For owls (definite evening):

Deep work	4 pm onwards
Shallow / Light work	1–4 pm
Rebound (for additional deep work)	10 am–1 pm

How a switch log will make you time wise

Do you ever get to the end of a workday and think to yourself, 'What did I actually do today?' And in response, you can't name a single thing?

If you work a standard 40-hour week, that's 2400 minutes to allocate to tasks. With so many minutes, it can be easy to be mindless about how you allocate your time at work. It's also easy to over-estimate the things you did spend time on, as well as the things you didn't. And this is exactly how Rahul Vohra, the founder and CEO of email software company Superhuman, arrived at the idea of using a switch log.

'Most people think they know how they spend their time, but they don't really,' Vohra explains. 'Sure, you have a calendar. But calendars are poor reflections of reality. Urgent tasks require our attention. Important work that we need to do might not even be on our calendars. And as the saying goes, you change what you measure.'

Vohra's question for himself morphed from 'How am I spending my time?' to 'How am I measuring my time?'.

The solution lies in the switch log. Vohra describes the switch log as being deceptively simple but surprisingly effective. 'Number one: log when you start a task. Number two: log when you switch tasks. And number three: log when you take a break. And here's the crazy part: after applying those rules, do whatever you want. Follow your intuition and do what seems important.'

Vohra uses a channel in Slack to log his time. Every time he begins a task, he sends a short message to himself in Slack. It will read TS (for Task Switch), colon, and then the name of the task. For example, 'TS: Calendar design review'. When he changes task, he does the same. And again, when he has a break. At the end of the day, he analyses how he used his time.

'The analysis itself is relatively simple. You take all your tasks and then you categorise them. My categories include product design, recruiting, PR, management, leadership, email and meditation. And then you just chart the time spent in each category.'

Vohra gave me an example of a week earlier in the year where upon analysing his switch log, he learned he had only spent 4 per cent of his time on recruitment and a whopping 22 per cent on public relations work. 'I know that as the CEO of a Series-B venture-backed company, I should be spending roughly 30 per cent of my time on recruiting. My own personal efforts on doing PR work is probably less important than hiring someone who can do that better than I could. And so I immediately found an actionable insight.'

Put it into action

1. Select software you will use to log your task switches. You might use Slack, like Vohra, or you could use Microsoft Excel or Google Sheets. You could even go old school and use pen and paper.
2. When you start a new task, enter TS: TASK NAME.
3. When you switch to a different task, repeat the process.
4. Continue to do this every single time you change tasks or take a break.
5. If you forget to log a task switch, it's usually obvious after about 5 or 10 minutes in that you find yourself doing a different task to what you wrote down. Simply go into your switch log, edit the task, and continue working.
6. Don't worry about updating your calendar to reflect your switch log – it doesn't matter if they match.

7. Take time at the end of the day or week to analyse your data. Do this by grouping all your tasks into categories and add up how much time you spent in each category. Ask yourself whether this reflects your values and priorities. If it does, then great! If it doesn't, think about what you can change about your behaviour in the weeks ahead to ensure better alignment.

8. If you are silently thinking to yourself (as I was when I first heard Vohra describe this strategy), 'This sounds like my idea of hell' – yes, there is a section of hell reserved especially for this strategy. And having applied it myself, it's horrible. But my goodness, it's worth the pain for the insights you get at the end.

Build a satisfying highlight into every day

Self-confessed productivity nerd and bestselling author of *Sprint* and *Make Time* Jake Knapp felt his to-do list was ruling his life. His days at Google, where he worked for over a decade, were ruled by this list. His life became all about getting to the end of it. But here's the unfortunate thing: to-do lists are never-ending. There is always more to do.

So Knapp began thinking differently about his day. Instead of obsessing over all the little tasks he wanted to get done, he started to largely ignore his to-do list. Instead, he focused on something completely different.

'Every day in the morning, I ask myself, "If the day was over, what would I want to say was the highlight of my day today? What would make me feel satisfied or feel joyful? What would that be?" So I think of one thing, not just one little task, but something more ambitious that might take me 60–90 minutes, and I write it down. I just write down that one thing.'

It doesn't mean Knapp won't do anything else. He still checks email and keeps a to-do list of smaller tasks. But instead of letting smaller things rule his day, the highlight becomes his priority.

'Instead of thinking, "I'm going to do a thousand things today", if I just do one thing that's really important, that's enough to be satisfied.'

After Knapp decides on his highlight, he timeboxes it in his diary. This action helps ensure it takes priority over everything else he could be doing.

Psychologists have found that the simple act of planning for or imagining a highlight in your day makes you more likely to fulfil your goals and be more resilient to challenges you might face during the day.

In one study led by Psychology Professor Gabriele Oettingen, a group of participants were asked to imagine a potential highlight of the day – namely, a creative task. They were asked to think about how they would feel if they thrived while doing it, as well as potential obstacles they may experience. A second group of people were asked to only imagine the highlight but not the obstacles, while a third group were just asked to consider the obstacles.

It turns out that envisaging a highlight – but also thinking about potential obstacles that might arise – led to the best performance of the task. When people thought about both the highlight and the challenges, they linked the positive emotions of the highlight with the obstacles they may encounter. And as such, when challenges did arise, people were able to feel excited about conquering them.

Now, being the Type A personality I am, I couldn't resist asking Knapp: Why not plan for two highlights? Surely two is better than one!

Knapp politely implied that I was missing the point. 'I think there is such a culture of busyness around most of us all the time at work and even outside of work. When I talk to other parents and I see how busy they are, it's everywhere. We're very busy people. And so the expectation is always to do more and more and more, and do it faster. And part of the idea with a highlight is to say, "Hey, it's okay to have one focal point and to do less but give it more energy".'

Thanks, Jake – the overachiever in me needed to hear that.

Put it into action

1. At the start of your workday, ask yourself: At the end of this day, what would I want to say the highlight of my day was? What would make me feel satisfied or joyful?

2. Ideally, pick something that will take you around 60–90 minutes to complete.
3. Block out that time in your diary, ideally for when you are at your peak energy (which, for most of us, is in the morning).
4. Prioritise getting your highlight done over anything else you have to do during the day.

How to do more $10,000 per hour tasks and fewer $10 per hour tasks

If you're like most people, you've probably broken down your annual salary into an hourly rate. Or if you're a business owner or freelancer, perhaps you've divided your annual revenue by the number of hours you work to get to a similar calculation. But have you ever thought about breaking down your day into the most valuable through to the least valuable tasks that you do?

World-renowned business strategist Perry Marshall has spent a lot of time thinking about hourly rates. Because for him, there is a completely different way of looking at this equation (and it has nothing to do with your ability to perform complex algebra).

Marshall gives the example of a receptionist, Helen, who works at a dental office for $15 per hour. 'Most of what Helen does is worth close to $0 per hour,' Marshall explains. 'But there are some things she does that are worth several thousand dollars an hour.'

'For example, imagine someone needs $5,000 of crowns and dental work. They search on Google and find the practice where Helen works. Helen answers their call but asks them to hold because she is busy with a customer. Two minutes later, she picks the phone back up and asks how she can help them. But they're gone. So they were going to spend $5,000 in two minutes, but the hold music scared them off and they're not coming back.'

'It took two minutes to lose $5,000.'

Everyone's workdays are full of high-value activities, along with less valuable activities. Marshall says we need to get better at identifying

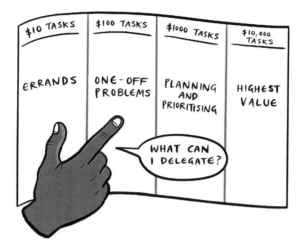

what are the $1,000 or $10,000 an hour tasks in our own work life and build more of them into how we structure our days.

But it's not enough to simply know which are the lower value activities. Once we have identified these tasks, Marshall says we need to find a way to reduce them or stop doing them altogether. This might involve delegating them to an assistant, for example, or outsourcing them to free ourselves up to spend more time on higher value activities.

Not all time is created equal. And if we can be more conscious about how we are using our time, we can spend it far more wisely.

Put it into action

1. Make a list of all the activities you do as part of your role, from small administrative duties through to more specialist activities.
2. Split these tasks into four columns:
   a) $10 per hour tasks (e.g. running errands, submitting your receipts to your accounts department, aligning diaries for a meeting)

b) $100 per hour tasks (e.g. helping a customer solve a one-off problem)

c) $1000 per hour tasks (e.g. planning and prioritising your week)

d) $10,000 per hour tasks (e.g. conducting sales meetings, solving a recurring customer problem)

3. See if you can delegate the $10 per hour tasks. For example, hire a virtual assistant, which typically costs between $5–10 per hour. If you can delegate four hours' worth of $10 per hour tasks and pay someone $40 in total to do that, imagine how much more value you could extract from your time if you filled those four hours with $1000 per hour tasks? You don't need a PhD in advanced statistical methods to know that this equals a lot more.

4. Apply the same thinking to your non-work life to outsource low value tasks that you can fill with higher value activities. In my own life, I've found someone on Airtasker to assemble IKEA furniture so I have more time for the higher value activity of building Harry Potter Lego with my seven-year-old daughter. (Or is that just my idea of awesome, high value time?)

It's time to prune bullsh*t from your diary

Take a look at your diary for this week. Are there meetings you have been invited to where you are unclear on their purpose or the role you are meant to play? Perhaps you have events coming up that you don't think you will particularly enjoy and you're not sure whether they will have a direct benefit on your career. Or maybe you blocked out time to produce a report that you have a sneaking suspicion that, God forbid, no-one will actually read?

If you answered 'yes' to any of these questions, chances are your diary could do with a prune.

Ashutosh Priyadarshy, founder of diary planning software company Sunsama, says it's easy to fill your workday with stuff that's only tangentially relevant or, worse, has no obvious connection to helping you achieve your goals. To optimise how he spends his days, Priyadarshy regularly removes what he refers to as 'bullsh*t' from his diary.

'I look at everything that I plan to do on a given day and I ask myself, "Is this thing obviously and directly correlated with the results that I want?" If it's two or three steps away from what I am focusing on, such as customer acquisition, that's usually a good indicator that it is probably bullsh*t.'

An example of this in Priyadarshy's life are networking events. While he might meet people at networking events who could help drive awareness and thus customer acquisition of Sunsama, it's far from guaranteed. 'I just try to do the things that feel so obvious and urgent and important, and forget about the rest.'

When I speak to my friends who work in large corporates and listen to them describing their workdays, I'm often struck by how much of their day could be classified as the bullsh*t Priyadarshy describes. So much 'work' is produced that has no impact on the goals of the organisation, and so many meetings happen that could have had fewer people attend or have been shorter and produced better outcomes.

For Priyadarshy, getting into the daily habit of planning his day the night before was what made him more conscious about pruning tasks, meetings and events from his diary. 'I think one of the really interesting things that happens when you plan your day regularly is that you build in these safety checks and it makes it harder for you to accept bullsh*t into your day.' And who doesn't want to have less bullsh*t to deal with every day?

Put it into action

1. Set aside time, ideally daily, to review your calendar.
2. For every meeting, event and timeboxed activity, ask yourself, 'Will this get me closer to achieving one of my goals?' If the answer is 'no', remove it from your diary. If the answer is 'yes', retain it. But if the answer is 'maybe' or 'indirectly', remove it. While this may feel uncomfortable at first, if you are able to fill this newfound time with activities that directly move you closer to your goals, you'll start to make quicker and more meaningful progress towards the things that matter.

How to stop people hijacking your calendar

John Zeratsky is obsessed with how he uses his time. For nearly 15 years, Zeratsky was a designer for technology companies such as Google and YouTube. He later moved to Google Ventures, where he worked with Jake Knapp on perfecting the Design Sprint – a time-constrained process to help companies generate and test new ideas. Zeratsky is also a self-confessed 'time dork' who wrote a book with fellow Googler Jake Knapp called *Make Time* about how to use time more effectively.

Something Zeratsky has given much thought to is his calendar structure. (Haven't we all? Okay, maybe that's just me and John). No matter what kind of an organisation you work for, chances are your co-workers can pop meetings into your diary at all times of day because it's visible to every single person in the business. Basically, anyone can hijack your day. How fun!

Unlike most of us, Zeratsky sees his calendar as an opportunity to think proactively, instead of reactively. He knows that a good day for him has several elements. It has time for deep work in the mornings, meals and breaks to keep him energised, administrative time for email and other tasks, exercise time, and time with his wife or friends.

The solution to proactively incorporate all these ingredients came to Zeratsky in the form of a calendar template.

'I actually use a calendar template inside Google Calendar,' he explains. 'It's not my primary calendar; it's a separate calendar that is the template of my ideal day. It has all of the building blocks – from when I eat, when my focused working blocks are, when I exercise – all those things.'

Zeratsky's day starts at about 6.30 am with a coffee, but without technology. 'It's important that I make coffee and have a few minutes to look out the window before I grab my phone or open up my computer. My wife and I set up a charging cabinet that all our devices go into at night. It creates this really nice barrier between us and technology. I have to make an intentional decision and say, "Okay, now I'm ready to begin the technology-focused part of my day".'

After coffee, Zeratsky works on his most important task for the day, typically something requiring deep, focused thinking. He also makes sure that he schedules in time for breaks and meals. 'I have found that when I don't do that, I have a tendency to get too into the zone when I'm doing focused work, and then I wait too long, and then I crash and burn. But if I schedule in breaks, it keeps me balanced.'

Administrative tasks and meetings happen in the afternoon. Zeratsky uses Calendly, the automated scheduling software, and programs his availability for meeting times to be in his afternoon block, typically between 2–5 pm. His exercise block follows at 5 pm, and then social time happens in the evening.

'I don't just play defence. I play offence,' summarises Zeratsky.

Put it into action

1. Think about all the ingredients for your ideal day. These might include time with family, exercise, focused work, meetings, emails, socialising with workmates or friends, meals and breaks, and so on.
2. Reflect on the time of day that is best suited to each activity.
3. Map out an ideal day. You could just focus on working hours or you could block out the entire day, like Zeratsky does.
4. When it comes to putting this in your calendar, there are two options. The first is taking Zeratsky's lead by using Google Calendar and creating a new calendar called Template.

This is a calendar that only you can see and you can switch the view on or off – essentially using it as a stencil to plan your day. Alternatively, you can use your actual calendar and block all activities into your calendar so that other people can't book over them. I've personally found that if I label things in CAPITAL LETTERS, colleagues take items in my diary more seriously, especially when I use unambiguous labels such as PLEASE DO NOT BOOK.

5. Wherever possible, try to plan your day according to your template.

How to make every hour productive

A great start to the day involves a protein-filled breakfast and doing your most important task first, right? Well, according to Brown University Economics Professor Emily Oster, that might not always be true (the task bit, not the breakfast).

When Oster considers how she will use the hours in her day, she applies an economics principle called 'optimising on the margin'. Before your eyes glaze over with the mention of economics terms (or maybe this is the highlight of the book for you?), let me explain what this means. The margin represents the current level of activity. And so to optimise on the margin, we need to consider what is the best use of the next hour instead of simply choosing activities based on how important they are.

'I try to make every hour as productive as possible,' describes Oster. 'And that means thinking about what the best use of that particular hour is given where I am on everything else, rather than saying all my time should be spent on this one big project.'

For example, Oster might have one work project that's much more important than another one. But when she thinks about making the most of the next hour, it would be best used on a smaller project because her brain is a bit foggy and she won't actually do great work on the more important but more demanding project.

When I interviewed Oster, I was in the middle of writing this book, so naturally, I asked her for advice on how I could apply this theory of optimising on the margin. She advised me to think about the diminishing marginal value of time spent writing my book every day. She assumed, correctly, that my first two hours of writing in the morning were very productive, but that it's downhill from there in terms of valuable writing produced. This is, sadly, very accurate.

'There's a temptation to think, "Okay, because this is so important, I have to push through", but actually, those additional hours are not that productive.' Oster suggested that at that point, I switch activities or even work on something administrative, because that will be the best use of the next hour: instead of pushing through for a third hour and having the quality and quantity of my output diminish considerably.

In other words, I am better off doing a completely different task in the next hour compared to pushing on with my book writing, given that an additional hour of book writing may be unproductive because I have reached my limit on that task. And through dedicating the next hour to a lower value task (i.e. something administrative) instead of having subpar performance on a higher value task, the decision actually leads to every hour being spent more wisely.

Put it into action

1. Resist adopting productivity advice that suggests you should prioritise your most important projects above all else. While you might start your day doing a few hours on your most critical project, check in with how you are feeling and be mindful of when you reach the point of diminishing returns.
2. At that point, deliberately swap tasks, potentially to something easier (and probably less 'important') to make the best use of the next hour. It is more valuable to work through less important administrative tasks, for example, than push on with your most important one but have the output be diminished because your energy is waning.

Stop treating breaks as an afterthought

Your calendar is probably littered with meetings. And by this stage in the book, you are hopefully blocking out time for deep work too (unless you just happened to have randomly opened the book on this page while browsing in a bookshop, in which case please return to GO and collect $200).

But do you also schedule breaks in your diary? If you're like most people, the answer is probably 'no'. Breaks are generally an afterthought – and something you do if and when you have a spare moment throughout the day.

Not only does professor and bestselling author of *Deep Work* and *A World Without Email* Cal Newport timeblock his entire day, he makes sure he schedules breaks in his diary.

'One of the reasons why people who timeblock get a productivity boost is that they timeblock their breaks,' explains Newport. 'It's a subtle psychological thing, but if you don't plan when your breaks are going to come, then any moment is potentially a time you could take a break. So what happens is all throughout the day, you have this argument with your mind: Should we take a break now? Should we jump on email now? Should we look on social media now? And if there's no pre-plan about when you're going to take those breaks, you're constantly having this argument.'

He says it's an argument people will lose more often than win and as a result, you end up fragmenting your attention much more. By booking breaks in your diary, you don't have to waste time arguing with yourself as to when you'll spend time away from your work.

At this point, you might be thinking, 'That's all well and good for Cal, but my diary is crazy! I have no time for breaks!' Well, the good news is that breaks don't need to be long. Research from the University of Colorado uncovered that there is an optimum length of time for breaks. The researchers found that in contrast to one 30-minute walking break, six 5-minute walking breaks boosted energy, sharpened focus, improved mood and reduced feelings of fatigue in the afternoon more effectively. Surely you can find a few 5-minute spots between all your meetings?

And in case those benefits are not compelling enough, a short break can also improve memory. In one study, after listening to a story, one group of people rested for 10 minutes while another group completed a task requiring intense concentration. Those who rested were more likely to remember the details of the story. This effect lasted for more than a week – all from the simple act of taking a short break.

Put it into action

1. Start by scheduling your most important break: lunch. To avoid having to manually do this every day, schedule at least 30 minutes for lunch as a recurring meeting with yourself so no-one can book over it (or if they do, your lunch appointment acts as a reminder to shift it to when you are not in a meeting). You can always shuffle the time around, but at least you know you'll have 30 minutes to yourself in the middle of every day.

2. Schedule short breaks throughout the day. They don't have to be more than 5 minutes long – but what matters is that they are regular.

3. Alternatively, use the 'speedy meetings' setting in Google Calendar, which makes the length of meetings default to 25 and 50 minutes, rather than 30 minutes and an hour. You will then have no excuse not to fit in 5-minute breaks into the structure of your day, even when you have back-to-back meetings.

How to avoid having a crazy busy day

You've probably had a workmate lament to you about their 'crazy busy' day. They probably told you they have back-to-back meetings and won't even have time to eat lunch. They joked about wishing they could consume food through an IV drip so as not to have to waste time eating (or is that just me who's had that thought?).

When we hear such claims, it's easy to falsely assume we must be talking to a Very Important Person, given they seem to be invited to so many meetings. We then question whether we should be trying to fill up our own diary with meetings to inflate our own sense of importance. Because it's natural to assume that the most successful people are booked solid for 100 per cent of their day.

The world's most successful people actually do the opposite when it comes to structuring their day.

Darren Murph is Head of Remote (yes, that's his actual job title) at software development company GitLab, the world's largest all-remote organisation. Gitlab has more than 1300 team members spread across nearly 70 countries, with no company-owned offices. Murph believes that being booked 100 per cent of the time is a huge risk.

'If you have your entire day pre-booked with meetings, it leaves no room whatsoever for real life to happen,' Murph explains. For example, you might get a call from your child's school saying you need to pick them up because they are sick. You might get an urgent request from a client that needs addressing straight away. Or a task you had planned to finish that day may have taken much longer than expected.

All of these scenarios could easily take you out for an hour or more, which not only impacts your own stress levels but also interferes with lots of other people's schedules too, especially if you are the back-to-back meetings type.

Murph points out that being booked for the entire workday can also have a detrimental impact on innovation. 'If you extrapolate that over an entire company where everyone is booked at 100 per cent, where's the room for ingenuity? Being booked at 100 per cent is a guarantee that your company is going to have no innovation and no serendipitous conversations because there's no time for that.'

So when you next meet someone who is complaining about their crazy busy, back-to-back meetings day, and you compare that against your less frantic and less occupied schedule, you can smugly think to yourself that, actually, you're probably the more successful one.

Put it into action

1. Instead of feeling a false sense of productivity if your diary looks full, deliberately schedule time to do nothing. Use these periods as 'buffer time' for things that run over, or for unexpected tasks that crop up during the day. You might even use this time for allowing creative and serendipitous things to happen. You could do this in one of several ways:
   - Schedule breaks into your calendar (which hopefully you are already doing, thanks to Cal Newport's advice – see page 74). It's important to protect time for recharging, and this time can also act as a buffer if meetings or other tasks take longer than expected.
   - When timeboxing, err on the side of overestimating how long something will take.
   - Schedule breathing space in between meetings. It doesn't have to be much, but having 5 or 10 minutes to action any quick items and read over your notes for the next meeting will make your day run smoother and help you feel more in control.

How to stop mindless email checking

Email is the Achilles heel of my productivity. While I have mastered not succumbing to social media distractions or getting sucked in by instant message pings, I do still manage to get lost in my inbox and use it as a semi-regular form of procrastination away from my 'real' work.

Despite spending so much time in my inbox and attempting to be an inbox-zero person (or at least inbox ten), I find this hard to achieve. There is so much procrastination joy to be had from mindlessly roaming around in there while achieving very little (although I do manage to also feel guilty just *thinking* about my bad email habits). Which is probably why I felt very excited hearing about John Zeratsky's approach to being more purposeful with his inbox.

Zeratsky used to work at Google Ventures and lead the creation of Design Sprints with Jake Knapp. Zeratsky thinks a lot about how he uses his time and, like me, he finds the temptation of his inbox hard to resist.

'I don't check email on my phone, but I do spend most of my day at a computer, which means temptation and access to email are always at hand,' he explains. To help mitigate the temptation, he batch processes his email. He does two quick reviews in the morning and a longer session in the afternoon. He even schedules time for it in his calendar.

Research by Kostadin Kushlev and Elizabeth Dunn from the University of British Columbia found that people who checked their email three times per day were significantly less stressed than those who constantly dip in and out. So in addition to working more productively, Zeratsky is doing wonders for his wellbeing with his email batching behaviour.

Outside of scheduling time for email, Zeratsky landed on a strategy that helped him be much more focused with the time he did spend in his inbox. And this is where I got really excited.

'I assign a purpose to each email session. The first is a strategy I call "fishing bear". During my morning email checks, I imagine myself as a fishing bear – standing on the bank of a river, reaching into the water to pluck out a tasty salmon here and there. I look for important and time-sensitive emails. If a message requires a quick reply, I write one. If it represents a chunk of work that needs to get done, I do it right away or put it on my calendar.'

During his fishing bear sessions, Zeratsky avoids trying to clear his inbox. This requires a different mindset. Which is where his afternoon sessions come in.

'In the afternoon, my energy is lower, my creativity is zapped, and it's a great time for what I call "munching cow". Like an energy-efficient cow chewing on grass, I methodically work my way through my inbox. Starting at the bottom, I read each message and reply, archive, or pull it out of my inbox.'

After being in munching cow mode, Zeratsky will conclude his afternoon session with a short burst of fishing bear to deal with anything time-dependent or important that arrived during the afternoon. He also doesn't aim for inbox zero every day. Instead, he prefers to do a full clean-up once every week or two.

The final part to Zeratsky's strategy involves recognising when an email isn't an email – when it's actually a task that is cleverly disguised as an email (I like to imagine an email wearing a sneaky little ninja mask). And this requires a different mindset.

'Sometimes I find myself with an important email stuck at the bottom of my inbox. Because it's important, I want to write a thoughtful response. But that takes time and focus, and my email sessions aren't optimised for that kind of deep work. The perverse result is that the most important stuff in my inbox is the least likely to get a proper and timely response.'

For Zeratskty, examples of these types of emails include providing feedback on a video, reviewing a legal agreement, creating a proposal for a new client. Basically anything that requires a decent chunk of time and headspace.

To overcome this problem, he takes these emails out of his inbox and schedules them in his diary so that the task actually gets done. And importantly, he allocates time for getting it done when he is in the headspace for deeper thinking work.

Put it into action

1. Book in dedicated time to check your emails, ideally three times per day.
2. Reflect on the different purposes you have when checking email. You might be like Zeratsky and have the two primary purposes: checking for and responding to important and urgent matters (fishing bear); and secondly, processing and clearing out your inbox (munching cow).
3. Set a purpose for your email sessions. You might borrow Zeratsky's names or you might dream up your own if you're not a fan of cows and bears.
4. Be sure to identify tasks that are disguised as an email. Move them out of your inbox and allocate time in your diary to actually doing them.

Why you need to finish your day with the Hemingway Trick

Some days, it can feel really hard to start work, especially work that requires deep, focused thinking. I had many moments while writing this book where I had a daily writing target to achieve but would instead sit staring at a flashing cursor for 20 minutes before something useful came out of my brain (although 'useful' might be overstating things on some mornings). All I wanted on these days was to get into flow and write, but my brain had other ideas.

Rachel Botsman, a world-renowned expert on trust and technology and the first ever Trust Fellow at Oxford University, used to love the 6–9 am slot for her writing. She found she could do more work in those three hours than she could achieve during the rest of the day. But when she had kids, that slot disappeared.

While trying to find a new groove for her work having started a family, she discovered that one of the tricks to getting into flow was how she settled herself in to work for the day. 'How you start is really key to the rest of the day,' Botsman explains.

'A really easy trick I learned is: if you're in flow the day before, don't finish that paragraph. Get halfway through the paragraph, and then stop. Write the next sentence the following day because it makes it really easy to pick up. Days where you've completed something, and you're starting again, they're harder because you're starting the engine from scratch.'

Organisational Psychologist and Wharton Professor Adam Grant uses a similar strategy. He refers to it as parking on a downhill slope, given the ease that this act brings to getting back into flow the following day.

Some people call this idea the Hemingway Trick. Writer Ernest Hemingway once said, 'When you are going good, stop writing.' Indeed, he was purported to have stopped each day's writing session halfway through a sentence. Author Roald Dahl also used the same strategy to avoid the terrifying blank page confronting him in his morning writing sessions.

Not only does finishing halfway through a task give us momentum, it has the added benefit of keeping the information in our brain. Psychologist Bluma Zeigarnik ran a famous experiment in 1927 where she observed that waiters were better able to remember complex orders when the order was interrupted or incomplete. However, as soon as the order was finished, it faded from memory more quickly. Known as the Zeigarnik Effect, this research demonstrates that our brain hates unfinished business, so much so that it will hold onto the information until it gets closure.

In the case of the Hemingway Trick, our brain continues to think about the unfinished task and when we come back to it, our brain is primed to easily pick back up where it left off.

Put it into action

1. When you are finishing work for the day, resist the temptation to reach a natural conclusion before clocking off. Instead, deliberately finish halfway through a sentence, a slide, a line of code, or whatever the type of work you are doing. By finishing halfway through, you'll find it far easier to get started the following day and have a much more time-wise morning.

It's time to start a 'quitting-time' ritual

My workday used to have several ends. I would end my day at the office by closing my laptop, packing it in my bag, and saying goodbye to my workmates. But after putting my daughter to bed, I would take my laptop back out of my bag and squeeze in a tiny bit of work before dinner. I'd close it again, eat my dinner, and return to my laptop. And finally, when my f.lux notification popped up to politely inform me that I needed to get off all devices to prepare for bed, I'd end my workday once more.

Not surprisingly, I never felt a sense of closure on my workdays. They simply blurred together. I felt like Bill Murray in *Groundhog Day*.

Things only got worse when I started working from home more frequently. It was just too easy to keep on working late into the evening.

Being deliberate about how we end our workday can have a hugely positive impact on how we feel about it – and how we feel about the next workday ahead of us. Yet I know I'm not alone in living the *Groundhog Day* experience when it comes to work, and in missing the opportunity to improve both engagement and productivity.

To help bookend her workdays, bestselling author and happiness guru Gretchen Rubin has a ritual she calls 'quitting time'. 'I will say to myself, "In 10 minutes it's quitting time and I'll take 10 minutes to tidy up my office",' explains Rubin.

'So if I got out papers, I'll put them back in a file or I'll put them back on my corkboard. I'll throw away my trash and I'll put my pens back in the pen cup.' For Rubin, it's not a deep clean, but more of a declutter and putting things back in their places.

Rubin finds that the '10-minute closer', as she sometimes calls it, clears her mind and acts as a transition out of work and into family life. And when she comes back to her home office in the morning, it feels easier to sit down and start work. 'I'm not finding my way through a bunch of papers or piles of books that I took notes on, or articles to read or just the stuff that accumulates.

'I like this ritual because for most people, and definitely for me, outer order contributes to inner calm.'

Psychologists have found that one of the biggest benefits of rituals such as this one is that they instil a sense of meaning in life. In one study, people were asked to write a diary of how they were feeling and the activities they did during the day. On the days people engaged in regular rituals and routines, they experienced a greater sense of meaning and purpose, which, in turn, improves resilience and determination. On the days when people did not engage in rituals or routines, they reported their life feeling more erratic or incoherent. Not surprisingly, they failed to experience the same level of meaning and purpose.

When it comes to the specific ritual of tidying up and putting things away, research published in *Psychological Science* suggests it's a highly beneficial ritual to adopt. In one study, participants had to write about a negative event, such as a decision they regretted, on a sheet of paper. Participants who then folded up this sheet of paper and placed it into an envelope felt their emotions improve. They felt relieved rather than anxious and experienced a sense of closure.

Just like the letter writers, the simple act of packing things away in your office at the end of a day – especially a challenging one – should provide an emotional boost and a sense of closure to your workday. And it will also mean you're not battling through a messy paper forest to get back to your computer in the morning.

Put it into action

1. At the end of your workday, take 5 to 10 minutes to reset your work area, whether this is at your office or at home.
2. Start with a physical clean-up. Put away stationery, files, coffee cups and other items that accumulate over the course of the day. (In my case, I would add Lego creatures, Hatchimals and things from the garden into the mix, as my daughter currently has a habit of bringing some very random things to my study.)
3. Next, do a digital clean-up. Shut the application windows you are finished with or the documents you left open during the day but can now close. And make sure you close your inbox so you are not tempted to start your day by checking it.

STRUCTURE
A summary

Work to your chronotype
Assess your chronotype: find out if you are a lark, middle bird, or owl. Use your chronotype's natural rhythm to help you decide when you should be doing focused, deep work and when you should be doing less cognitively demanding work.

The switch log
Log your task switches. When you start a new task, enter TS: TASK NAME. When you switch to a different task, repeat the process. Continue to do this every single time you change tasks or take a break. Analyse your data at the end of the week and ask yourself whether how you used your time reflects your priorities. If there is a mismatch, think about what you can change about your behaviour to ensure better alignment.

Schedule a highlight
At the start of your workday, ask yourself: At the end of this day, what would I want to say the highlight of my day was? Ideally, pick something that will take you around 60–90 minutes to complete. Block out that time in your diary, ideally for when you are at your peak energy. Prioritise getting your highlight done over anything else you have to do during the day.

Do more $10,000 per hour tasks

Make a list of all the activities you perform as part of your role, from minor administrative duties through to more specialist tasks. Split these into four columns: $10 per hour tasks, $100 per hour tasks, $1000 per hour tasks, and $10,000 per hour tasks. Think about how you can delegate the $10 per hour tasks to free up more time to do higher value tasks.

Remove bullsh*t from your diary

Set aside time, ideally daily, to review your calendar. For every meeting, event and timeboxed activity, ask yourself, 'Will this get me closer to achieving one of my goals?' If the answer is 'no', remove it from your diary. It's probably bullsh*t.

Create a calendar template

Think about all the ingredients (work and non-work) for your ideal day. Reflect on the time of day that is best suited to each activity. Map out an ideal day by creating a calendar template in Google Calendar and blocking out each activity in the template. This is a calendar that only you can see. Use it as a stencil to plan your day.

Optimise on the margin

While you might start your day doing a few hours on your most critical project, check in with how you are feeling and be mindful of when you reach the point of diminishing returns. At that point, deliberately swap tasks to something easier (and probably less 'important') to make the best use of that hour. It is more valuable to work through less important administrative tasks, for example, than push on with your most important task but have the output be diminished because your energy is waning.

Schedule short and long breaks in your diary

In your diary, schedule lunch (at least 30 minutes) and several short breaks (5–10 minutes) throughout the day. By scheduling breaks, you will stop wasting mental energy deciding when to take a break.

Don't book yourself at 100 per cent

Instead of feeling a false sense of productivity if your diary looks full, deliberately schedule time to do nothing. You can use this as 'buffer time' for things that run over, or for unexpected tasks that crop up during the day. Or you can even use it for allowing creative and serendipitous things to happen.

Assign a purpose to email checking

Book in dedicated time to check your emails. Reflect on the different purposes you have when checking email, such as identifying and responding to important and urgent matters (fishing bear), and processing and clearing out your inbox (munching cow). Set a purpose for your email sessions. Also, be sure to identify tasks that are disguised as an email. Move them out of your inbox and allocate time to doing them in your diary.

The Hemingway trick

When you are finishing work for the day, deliberately finish halfway through a sentence, a slide, a line of code or whatever the type of work it is you are doing. By finishing halfway through, you'll find it far easier to get started the following day.

Create a quitting-time ritual

At the end of your workday, take 5–10 minutes to reset your work area, whether this is at your office or at home. Start with a physical clean-up such as putting away stationery, files and coffee cups. Next, do a digital clean-up by closing the application windows you are finished with or the documents you left open during the day. Finally, make sure you close your inbox so you are not tempted to start your day by checking it.

EFFICIENCY
Work faster and smarter

Have you ever got to the end of the day and thought to yourself, 'Wow! I have a couple of excess hours that I have no idea how to spend!' Of course you haven't! There are never enough hours in the day, right? Wrong. This next part of the book will help give you back precious time in your day.

We are going to head into the world of zombies, mice and robots. No, this section is not about a pending apocalypse. It's about efficiency. It's about how to make the most of the time you have and find a few shortcuts along the way.

One of the best ways to be more efficient is to kill things. I'm not talking about actual murder. Specifically, we are going to kill some zombies. You'll then learn how to turbocharge the speed at which you do things using the power of automation.

Meetings are one of the biggest efficiency buzzkills out there, so, naturally, this section will provide several different strategies to keep your meetings lean, efficient and impactful, including when to schedule them, what to do during them, and who to invite (or not invite).

We are then going to whip your inbox into shape and look at the power of constraints when it comes to being smarter with your time. Finally, you'll learn about what mice have to do with productivity.

Why you need to go on a zombie hunt

Do you have zombies at your workplace? Are reawakened corpses that smell like rotting flesh stalking your office building?

Okay, so perhaps the walking dead haven't literally invaded your workplace, but metaphorically, they might have.

Global Innovation Thought Leader and Senior Partner at growth strategy consulting firm Innosight, Scott D. Anthony, thinks a lot about zombies. More specifically, he thinks a lot about zombie projects.

'A zombie project is like the walking undead,' explains Anthony. 'It is the shuffling, lingering project that, if you are honest about it, will never have material impact. But it's the thing that is sucking all the innovation life out of an organisation. It's the thing that's killing your ability to do new things because you're working on all these zombie efforts that are taking all of your time and all of your energy.'

So why are there so many zombie projects? Perhaps not surprisingly, research has found that people do not like to believe their past choices were misguided. We want to assume that we were indeed being clever to select the projects that now occupy our time. So when we discover that one of the projects we are working on is not particularly valuable, we convince ourselves that we simply need to devote even more time to this task or goal – because surely that will make it better! Psychologists call this escalation of commitment.

Anthony has found the zombie idea really resonates inside large companies because there is such a stigma about raising your hand and saying, 'You know that idea that we've spent 12 months and millions of dollars working on? Well, it's actually not producing any value and we should probably stop working on it.'

But putting zombies out of their misery is easier said than done.

As well as helping clients identify and kill zombies, Anthony has killed many in his own working life. And several years ago, he had the perfect opportunity to do so when he transitioned from being the Managing Partner of Innosight and handed the role to one of his US colleagues.

'It was a great moment because it allowed me to step back and look at my calendar and ask, "Which of the regular standing meetings that I have with colleagues are really things that are great investments of my time for both me and the other person? Which are ones that have just become routines that we did because the calendar told us that we should meet every X number of weeks?"'

Through asking these questions, Anthony was able to remove between 50 and 70 per cent of zombie meetings from his diary. And what's more: no one really noticed because the meetings were adding so little value to their work.

One such meeting that he was able to eliminate was a recurring operations meeting with a colleague with whom he had worked for over a decade. 'We had a standing update call, and we would dutifully try to find agenda items to go through, but it turned out that Jeanne and I could handle those agenda items really well by email. So we stopped having the calls and we started doing email updates instead. It allowed both of us to save time and it didn't impair the effectiveness of either one of us.'

Put it into action

1. Take a look at your diary and work activities for the next fortnight. Alternatively, you might want to reflect on the fortnight just finished.
2. Ask yourself: What are the projects that I'm working on and the routine meetings that I have that don't have a purpose

any more or are not creating value? For recurring meetings, ask yourself, 'Does it make sense for us to be meeting at this frequency?' or 'Can this meeting be done just as well via asynchronous updates (meaning non-live communication, such as email and instant messaging)?'

3. Kill your zombies by eliminating those projects, activities and meetings.

4. For additional zombie-killing tips or to help launch a zombie-killing campaign in your team or organisation, go to amantha.com/timewise for more resources.

Stop wasting time on repetitive tasks

There are some aspects of my job that I find incredibly tedious. One of those activities is uploading podcast episodes to the software platform that distributes *How I Work* to all the podcast apps. It's a weekly task, and while it only takes about 15 minutes per week, it was something I would always put off until the last minute.

One day, when I was executing this administrative task, I had a brainwave: I could give the task to someone else to do instead! And this is exactly what Cal Newport would have recommended that I do.

'There is a standard idea from outsourcing thinking that if you're going to do something more than thirty times a year, then it's worth automating or outsourcing,' Newport told me. 'It's called the 30x rule. If you're going to do a task that many times, then the overhead of figuring out how to outsource or automate it will probably generate a positive return.'

For my podcast process, I decided to outsource this task to Inventium's Virtual Assistant, Elaine. This meant an investment of around an hour where I wrote out the process into a document. Elaine now relieves me of this task every single week, and for that I am both very grateful and have a bonus 15 minutes in my week.

Despite not being able to write code, I am also a big fan of automation. In my inbox, I have an automated process that directs certain e-newsletters that I love to read, but read in batches, into a specific inbox called 'read later'. Learning how to automate this process and setting it up took me about half an hour, but over the course of a year, it probably saves me hours of time spent manually moving or filing hundreds of emails that come into my inbox.

Another area of my work life in which I have invested time in automation is in responses to common emails I receive. For example, I'm sent anywhere between two and ten enquiries from people wanting to be a guest on *How I Work* every single day. I only accept about one in fifty of these pitches. As such, I found myself writing countless rejection emails until it dawned on me that I could automate this task. So I created an email template (what Gmail calls a 'canned response') that provides a polite rejection. I can send it with the press of two keys on my keyboard, instead of spending a few minutes typing several sentences to each individual person.

Put it into action

1. Over the course of a week (or even two), make a note of all the activities you do at work that are repetitive. You could use the 30x rule to guide you, in that if you do the task or activity more than thirty times in a year, you could classify it as repetitive.
2. Think about whether the activity is best suited to being outsourced or automated. Activities that lend themselves to automation include tasks that require a lot of copying and pasting (such as creating reports), sorting things into categories (triaging your inbox), scheduling meetings, making payments – basically anything that is (or can be) rule-based. Conversely, any process that is repetitive but does not always follow the exact same rules or needs a human touch is more suited to outsourcing.
3. For automating activities, you might want to research software that can help. At the time of writing, I have found Zapier to be useful in automating processes that require two different software programs to speak to each other. And Keyboard Maestro is excellent automation software for Mac users.

4. For outsourcing activities, there might be someone in your organisation to whom you could give tasks. Alternatively, at Inventium, we found having a virtual assistant to be a cost-effective solution for outsourcing a lot of administrative and repetitive work.

Why you need to say 'no' to coffee meetings

Carolyn Creswell, founder of Carman's Kitchen (also known as the maker of my daughter's favourite muesli bars), gets asked out for coffee a lot. Many wannabe entrepreneurs are keen to pick her brain and receive advice from Creswell, who is one of the most successful female entrepreneurs in Australia.

'When I started the business, I was working crazy hours,' Creswell recalls. 'I was working late at night and there was always stuff to do on weekends. What I realised over a period of time is that if someone comes up to you on the street and says, "Can I have $20?" you say "no". But if someone says, "Can I have 20 minutes or can I have a coffee with you?" you feel like you have to say "yes".'

Saying 'yes' to requests on our time is so easy to do. And because it's time, not money, it feels as if it doesn't cost us anything. But assuming the coffee is work-related, and if you were to work out your hourly rate, it *does* cost you. In addition, the time you spend meeting someone for a coffee means you might have to find time to do your actual job after hours.

For Creswell, she is genuinely keen to help – but not at the expense of maintaining work–life balance and prioritising time with her family when she is not in the office. For her, saying 'yes' to a coffee can mean the difference between getting to 5:30 pm and feeling like everything is under control and she can leave in time to have dinner with her family, or not.

'I will happily help someone, so often on the drive to work or home from work, I'll have a mentoring call. But when someone gets in touch to ask if we can have a coffee, I'll start by saying, "Can we just have a phone call?" I'll book it in, so they know that at 9 am on Tuesday the 19th, I'll be calling them. But I only book calls for the dead time when I'm driving to or from work.'

Given Creswell generally doesn't meet with people externally, filling what would otherwise be unproductive time while in the car means she is able to spend this time helping others. 'That's my way of juggling it, so that I can not feel like I'm giving everything to everyone else and I can't actually get my own work done.'

As someone who receives a lot of emails from people wanting to meet for coffee and 'pick my brain', I adopted Creswell's advice as soon as I heard it. If I do end up saying 'yes' to someone (and I mostly say 'no'), I'll always schedule it for time when I am in the car or will be on one of my daily walks.

Put it into action

1. When you next receive a request for a coffee, reflect on whether you really want to say 'yes'. Sure, there might be some people you genuinely do want to meet, but there will be other times when you are only saying 'yes' out of obligation.
2. If you do genuinely want to help the other person, schedule a phone chat for a time that would otherwise be dead time, such as during your commute or a daily walk.

How to dramatically reduce your meeting load

A couple of years ago, as part of his quarterly performance review with himself, Dom Price was reflecting on the way he was working. Price, who heads up Research and Development and is the resident Work Futurist at Atlassian, attends a lot of meetings. And he was thinking about how much he loathed attending meetings (like every other human being on the planet).

'I was drowning in meetings, forums, committees, catch-ups, councils, groups, squads, tribes,' Price recalls. 'I felt like everyone was wanting a little bit of me.'

At the same time, Price was trying to work out how to free up more time to do more of what he loved – coaching and mentoring others. But his plate was full. So he tried something rather extreme: Price deleted every single meeting from his calendar, accompanied by a note to the meeting organiser that offered one of three options.

Option 1 asked the meeting organiser to respond with the purpose of the meeting, Price's role and responsibility in the meeting, and what specifically they wanted Price to add to it.

Option 2 asked the organiser to defend the purpose of the meeting and suggest who from Price's team could attend in his place.

Option 3 suggested that Price or one of his team didn't need to attend the meeting, or conversely, that the meeting didn't even need to be held. 'They're the meetings that probably shouldn't exist and they just kind of do. And with this approach, over one-third of meetings just never came back to my diary. The meeting only existed because it existed last year. Because you never kill a meeting, you only ever add a meeting.'

Not only did this strategy liberate much of Price's diary, but he was also then able to attend the meetings that did remain knowing his exact role and responsibilities. Price reported that simply requesting the meeting organiser clarify his role led to a huge reduction in his cognitive load (not to mention making the time spent in meetings much more efficient and effective). He now knew whether he was there to challenge, contribute, be a provocateur or something else entirely.

'If you've not articulated my role, I'm going to guess why I am there and chances are, I'll get it wrong. And I had. I was on autopilot because I had too many meetings. So now I have less meetings and the ones I have are focused on something specific, and I believe that my contribution in those meetings has now increased. And then I've carved out that free time for doing the thing which I love, which is coaching and mentoring.'

Put it into action

1. Delete every meeting in your diary and accompany the deletion with a note to the organiser, providing them with three options.
   - Option 1 is that they re-invite you to the meeting but specify the purpose of the meeting and the role they want you to play.
   - Option 2 is that someone else can sub in for you and you don't have to attend.
   - Option 3 is that you don't need to be at the meeting anymore, or better still, that the meeting doesn't even need to exist.

Stop wasting everyone's time – including your own

In 2018, Andrew Barnes' estate planning company, Perpetual Guardian, made headlines around the world for permanently introducing a Four-day Week (FDW). The concept of a FDW can be summed up as 100 per cent pay for 80 per cent time at work, on the condition that 100 per cent of agreed productivity is achieved. In a nutshell, staff work four normal eight-hour days, provided they achieve what they would in a normal five-day week. And they get paid a full-time salary. It's like work utopia. But it's actually real.

When Barnes made the move to the FDW, he knew things had to change. 'There's not just personal responsibility about how you use your own time,' explained Barnes. 'You also have to think about how you waste other people's time, because if I waste a whole pile of people's time in my team by inviting them to a meeting that they don't need to be at, and then as a consequence we don't achieve our productivity outcomes, that puts everybody's Four-day Week in jeopardy as a team. So it's two-way: I'm not going to waste your time and you don't waste mine.'

Implementing rules around meetings was one way to help people think twice about how they could use their own time and other people's time more efficiently. As an example, meetings at Perpetual Guardian were typically all one hour long. Barnes admitted there was no reason for meetings to default to one hour other than the fact that online calendars default to this length.

To help protect people's time, staff introduced the rule that meetings could be no longer than 30 minutes. 'This means several things have to change in how meetings are run. You've got to have an agenda. You've got to be focused. You can't just drag on for the sake of it.'

In addition, because of the focus on productivity and outcomes, staff were given explicit permission to pick and choose which meetings they attend. 'If it's not relevant, don't attend it. This rule stops the mass meetings where everybody shows up, nobody says anything, and nobody really gets anything out of it.'

The FDW forced employees to think carefully and deliberately about how they spent their time. If you attend every meeting you are invited to, you're possibly not going to get your work done in four days. You may have to work five. So having this constraint challenged everyone to ask how important each meeting was for delivering their goals.

Barnes' rules around meetings and respecting people's time were echoed in Japan when Microsoft introduced a FDW trial. They had three rules. First, you had to use Microsoft Teams for meetings. Second, no meeting could be longer than half an hour. Third, no more than five people could be invited to a meeting. Productivity went up by 39.9 per cent based on these three rules alone. I suspect happiness skyrocketed, too.

Put it into action

1. Before booking a meeting and inviting other people, ask yourself 'Does every individual really need to attend?'
2. Think about capping the length of meetings and the number of people allowed to attend each meeting.
3. Finally, let meeting attendance be the decision of the attendee. Give people permission to decline meetings if they feel that they can't contribute or attending the meeting won't contribute to achieving their goals.

It's time to replace meetings with videos

How many meetings have you sat in over the last month that consisted of someone giving an update of their work? If you're like most people, probably quite a few. And chances are, you've also spent valuable time in meetings where you were on the receiving end of information, as opposed to being an active participant. Meetings like these not only eat up a lot of valuable work time but also interrupt the flow and efficiency of our days. They are also pretty dull (unless someone has brought doughnuts, in which case they are marginally better).

Job van der Voort is the co-founder and CEO of Remote.com, a company that helps businesses employ global talent legally and easily. It will probably come as no surprise that Remote.com is a remote-first organisation, meaning no-one is expected to work from a physical office in a central location.

Van der Voort has thought a lot about meetings and how to improve them, which is critical in a business like his where staff work all over the world in a variety of different time zones. At Remote.com, communication defaults to asynchronous – meaning non-live communication such as email. And while some meetings still take place, including a regular all-staff meeting, Remote.com employees try to avoid scheduling long or recurring meetings.

Remote.com's regular all-staff meeting is only 30 minutes long. But what makes it particularly unique is that instead of leaders and teams giving live updates, everything is recorded on video in advance.

'People post their updates in a central location, which will be a video or sometimes just a short, written update. People tend to stick to, at most, 5 minutes, so they are really short updates that give the ability to quickly see what is happening across the organisation,' explains van der Voort. Updates are categorised by department, so if you started at Remote.com a couple of days ago and you want to see what is happening in the sales department, you can simply log on to the intranet and watch that particular video.

Van der Voort admits it took quite a while to encourage everybody to start recording their updates. 'Now that people are doing it consistently, it's an incredible source of information because it moves away from the requirement of having to search deeply through documentation just to get a glance of the current status of things. Instead, you can just watch a video or even just read the transcript and it still gives you somewhat of a personal touch because you can put a face to a department or a face to a particular task.'

In addition to being an effective way to share information, especially for those working across different time zones, creating video recordings often replaces the need for meetings at Remote.com. 'I had a new colleague start working with me yesterday,' van der Voort explains. 'Instead of setting up an hour-long meeting, I just recorded a bunch of videos.'

Put it into action

1. Before scheduling a meeting, think about whether it could be replaced with the recording of a video or by providing an email update (and chances are, a lot of the time, it probably could be). Alternatively, you might want to do a combination of both: prepare a video that people can watch in their own time and then review anything that warrants discussion during the meeting.

2. Choose a program that enables you to record a video easily. At the time of writing, Loom is the software used by

Remote.com staff. With Loom, you can record a video of your screen, you can record a video of yourself, or you can capture a combination of the two where you see a window on your computer and a little image of you talking.

3. Share all videos in a central repository, such as your organisation's intranet. This allows anyone to be able to get an update at a time that works for them.

Win back time through meeting batching

It's Tuesday afternoon and you have a meeting coming up in 40 minutes. You are drowning in work but can't decide how best to use your time before it begins. You consider starting work on a big sales presentation you have to deliver tomorrow, but decide against it because you don't want to get into flow, only to be interrupted by this meeting. You think about a few other meaty tasks you need to complete but you tell yourself they're not worth starting because you need at least an hour to really get stuck into them.

You haphazardly go through your inbox, making a small amount of progress on tasks that are essentially meaningless but feel good in the moment. You delete a bunch of random newsletters you didn't even know you'd subscribed to, you skim some emails that you really didn't need to be cc-ed on (and have now wasted precious time reading), and you scan over some old emails you had meant to action but ran out of time.

You look at the clock – it's time for your meeting! And lo and behold, you have also just managed to waste 40 minutes of your day.

Batch-checking email – whereby you only check emails two to three times per day – has become a common productivity tip. Batching meetings can have an equally big impact on our efficiency.

Research from Ohio State University has shown that when you have a meeting coming up in the next hour or two, people get 22 per cent less work done compared to if there was no upcoming meeting.

It's hard to get into flow when you know you have a major interruption just around the corner.

This study happens to be one of Adam Grant's favourites. He found it affirming for the way he deliberately structures his days at university. 'On a teaching day, I hold all my office hours [meetings with students] back-to-back. I learned that I needed a little buffer, so that might be 5 minutes between each meeting just to catch up on email or in case a meeting ran longer than expected.' Grant then contrasts his office-hours days with days that have no meetings scheduled when he can really focus and be productive on his research and writing.

Put it into action

1. Consider creating rules for yourself for when you don't schedule or accept meetings. For example, if you are most cognitively sharp in the mornings, implement a 'no meetings' rule for several mornings per week. You could achieve this by batching your meetings in the afternoon.

2. If you have minimal control over your calendar, speak to your boss and other people who put meetings in your diary about the productivity gains that can come from batching meetings. Instead of implementing 'no meetings' blocks of time in your diary, try the reverse: create blocks of time during the week that are dedicated to meetings. For example, 1–3 pm, when our brains tend to be a bit foggy, are a great time for meetings that are less cognitively demanding such as work-in-progress meetings or daily stand-ups.

A formula for more efficient meetings

Rahul Vohra, founder and CEO of email software company Super-human, believes that most teams run inefficient meetings. He says that agendas are often non-existent, or very loose at best. Certain topics are discussed to the exclusion of others. Too much time is spent talking about unimportant issues, while other, more important, problems are starved of attention and can persist for weeks at a time without anyone paying attention to them.

Vohra says there are three ingredients for making meetings at Superhuman as efficient and impactful as possible. The first rule is that if somebody wants to raise a topic for discussion in a team meeting, they must write it down beforehand and share it with the team by 6 pm the day before.

'We should avoid talking about things that were not written down, because we can read much faster than we can speak,' explains Vohra. 'If you're spending your team meeting just communicating ideas, that's obviously inefficient because you could have written it down and everyone could have read it beforehand.' And in addition to speed, talented talkers will inadvertently (or perhaps deliberately) bias people towards their ideas, thus disadvantaging those who do not have the gift of the gab.

Vohra's second rule is that if somebody wants to contribute during a team meeting, they must have read and commented on the documents beforehand. He sees this strategy as not only a time efficient one, but also one of respect.

'We should avoid commenting on things where we did not invest the time to get up to speed as it needlessly wastes the time of those who did. It's not enough for someone just to write a document saying, "This is the problem. This is the solution," and have only half the team read it. If that's the case, and sometimes it is because certain weeks are busier than others, then those who have not read it are not parties to that discussion. As a result, this keeps things moving very quickly.'

According to research, this part of Vohra's strategy should lead to better decision-making. While many people believe that our gut instinct tends to be accurate, it turns out we are better served with a bit more reflection time.

In a study led by Professor Justin Kruger from New York University's Stern School of Business, the researchers were curious to know if students' initial answers to multiple-choice tests were more accurate than those who had changed their mind. The researchers homed in on the instances in which students had erased their initial answer.

Kruger and his colleagues found that when students returned to their original answer, their responses were more likely to be wrong – this is known as the First Instinct Fallacy. Whereas if they did not return to the original answer, their responses were more likely to be correct. This data raises two issues. First, giving people additional time, as Vohra does, to contemplate their decisions prior to a meeting will lead to better decision-making and avoid people falling victim to the First Instinct Fallacy (when people are asked to make decisions on the spot). And second, how did I not know about this study when I was going through the torture of doing multiple choice tests during my university days?

The final rule for successful and efficient meetings is that if something is discussed in the team meeting, it is discussed for 5 minutes at most. If consensus is not reached within five minutes, then the conversation stops, and a decision-maker is identified.

Vohra classifies decisions into reversible and non-reversible decisions. Reversible decisions have lower stakes. If a poor decision is made, it is easy to pivot and take the other path. Non-reversible decisions have higher stakes and can be costly to a business if the wrong one is made.

As the CEO, Vohra makes all non-reversible decisions. All reversible decisions are delegated to a member of his team, a great way of empowering his staff, which would presumably have flow-on effects to their overall job satisfaction. 'After the meeting, the decision maker will gather all the required information and they make the decision before the next team meeting.' This avoids the tendency for people to avoid actually making decisions, especially hard ones.

'We found that by applying these tactics, everyone is always up to speed. Each item takes 5 minutes at most, and in 1 hour, you can get through ten items with tonnes of room for fun and banter along the way.'

Put it into action

1. For team meetings, ask team members to add anything they want to discuss to a written agenda in a shared document at least one day prior to the meeting. Ask people to specify what they want to talk about and any background reading necessary, so the team can get up to speed. While you may initially come across as the Mussolini of Meetings, your team members will thank you for it when they realise you are creating efficient meetings.

2. Ask all team members to read the agenda and any pre-reading associated with the different topics for discussion.

3. In the meeting, only allow people who have read the pre-reads to comment.

4. If decisions are not made after 5 minutes of discussion, the leader should take responsibility for making any non-reversible decisions. Reversible decisions should be delegated to someone on the team. All decisions should be made before the next team meeting.

5. For the next meeting, add items to the agenda where a decision needs to be made to ensure decision-making doesn't drag on.

Why you need a 'To Discuss' list

If you're familiar with Agile methodology, you're probably good friends with kanban boards. As a quick refresher, a kanban board is a simple chart to help visualise the workflow for a project. At its most basic, a kanban board has three columns: To Do, Doing, Done. All tasks associated with a project start in the To Do column, and gradually make their way across to the Done column.

Georgetown University Professor Cal Newport is a big fan of the kanban board. He has several boards for the different roles in his life. He has a board for his writing, his computer science research, his university administration work, and for his role as the Director of Graduate Studies. I also like to secretly imagine that he uses one to keep track of household chores at home with his kids (although if I were to apply this to my own home life with my daughter, I suspect that 'tidy up bedroom' would rarely make it to the Done column).

While using kanban boards for individual project management is not a novel idea (Google 'personal kanban' for inspiration), what I found most interesting were the task categorisations Newport uses.

For Newport's role as Director of Graduate Studies, which involves coordinating between, and talking to, lots of different people, he has a column labelled To Discuss. 'I realised I could save a tonne of email communication through having a To Discuss column,' Newport explained to me on *How I Work*. Every time Newport had something he needed to ask his department chair or program administrator or anyone else he was working with, he resisted the urge to just shoot off an email in that moment. Instead, he listed the topic for discussion on his board.

'While sending an email in the moment would give me a little bit of relief, every one of those is a new unscheduled message that's out there and a new unscheduled response. That's then going to potentially lead to a long back and forth chain of unscheduled messages, which I learned doing the research for my book, *A World Without Email*, is productivity poison.'

Newport ended up creating To Discuss columns for several people with whom he frequently needed to talk through important issues. Then, whenever he was next meeting with them, he was able to plough through the topics for discussion swiftly and resolve them instantly – a much wiser and more efficient use of time. 'This probably saved me many dozens of unscheduled emails per week by just waiting until I got to those next meetings. So it was a great productivity saver for that particular role.'

Now, you might be reading this and thinking, 'But it's so much more convenient to just fire off an email', especially if the matter is urgent. However, Newport argues that we overestimate what urgent actually means.

'Often, when people think they need a response now, it's because they don't want to keep track of it. "I want a response now because I don't know if you're going to answer or not and I'm not organised enough to keep track of whether I have heard back from Cal about this. So I'm going to send you this email and just get a response right away so I can take this off the things I need to worry about."'

Utilising a To Discuss column will help you keep track of what you need to ask other people, as well as removing the impulse to send emails that feel urgent but in fact create more work and don't actually get you closer to resolving issues.

Put it into action

1. Create a new section on your to-do list called To Discuss. Alternatively, if you are a fan of kanban boards, add a To Discuss column alongside To Do, Doing and Done. You might even set up several different To Discuss lists based on all the people you communicate with frequently.
2. Take out your To Discuss list when you are meeting with the person and work through everything on the list. If you don't have a meeting scheduled, wait until you have a few items on your list before booking a meeting together.

Treat your email like your laundry

When Laura Mae Martin started work at Google more than a decade ago, she began work on the 20% Project, whereby Google employees can spend one day per week on a self-set project. Martin used this time to develop an internal training program on how to manage your inbox effectively (hello, dream job!). She ended up running this program for thousands of Googlers. Martin then parlayed this passion project into the full-time role of Executive Productivity Advisor (okay, this is seriously my dream job), where she works one-on-one with executives at Google to help them work more productively.

Martin likens email to doing your laundry. 'Pretend that your dryer is your inbox. Imagine how most people are doing email right now: they go in, they grab one shirt, they fold it, and they walk it all the way up to their dresser, and then they walk all the way back down.

'Then maybe they find a pair of pants and they are still wet, and they think, "Oh, I'll just throw it back in there with all of my dry clothes." In their inbox, maybe that's marked as unread because you don't want to deal with it right now. Then you find one sock, but you don't know where the other sock is, but you put it away anyway, knowing you're going to have to go back. And by the end of it, you're like, "I'm just going to start the dryer all over and look at it again tomorrow".'

Martin explains that the reason email is the source of so much stress is because people approach their inbox in this manner. They pick and choose. Instead, Martin says people need to approach email like they do their dryer. Decide that it's time to empty the dryer,

get everything out, put things into piles, fold things, and then put them away.

For Martin, being in her inbox is a deliberate choice, as opposed to something she aimlessly cruises around in during the day. And to make herself more productive, she has a very specific workflow she uses when looking at her emails.

The first thing Martin does is process all incoming emails, which she sorts into one of three piles (or, in the case of Gmail, tabs or multiple inboxes). The first pile is To-Do – things she needs to action personally that don't require input from anyone else. The second pile is To-Do – Waiting, which are things she has to do but needs to wait for someone's input or response before she can do them. The final pile is emails that she has to Read.

Martin's day starts with opening her inbox and getting to zero through sorting any incoming emails in chronological order. 'I use something called auto-advance. It forces me to go to the next email versus going back to the dryer and picking out whatever I want that looks shiny.' Each email is then sorted into one of her three piles or it gets archived.

When working through her three piles, Martin matches her energy to the task. 'If I have two hours of uninterrupted time, I know that

I can dive into some of those To-Dos, so I open that folder only and I don't look at the rest of my inbox. I just turn to the clothes I need to fold and I go through each one of them and fold, fold, fold.' Kind of like a domestic goddess, but for email.

In the afternoon, when her energy is a bit lower, Martin uses this time to go through her Read folder. And at the end of the day, she will go to her To-Do – Waiting folder and check if there is anything holding up her progress that could be bumped up right now, or anything that has a deadline and needs to be chased.

Martin says she only has two rules when it comes to email. 'Treat it like laundry and close it once or twice a day. I don't recommend that you only look at your email once because for a lot of people, that's just not realistic. You're going to miss something for the next meeting, for example. So it can be open but close it if you've set time to work.'

Put it into action

1. Create multiple inboxes in your email labelled To-Do, To-Do – Waiting, and Read.
2. When you go into your inbox for the first time during the day – or alternatively, you can do this right at the end of your day – sort all your emails into those three folders.
3. Pick a time of the day when you are feeling energetic to go through your To-Do pile.
4. When you are feeling less energetic, go through your Read pile.
5. Once every day or two, go through your To-Do – Waiting pile and see if you need to chase anything up.
6. Aim to close your inbox at least once a day when you need to have some uninterrupted time to do deep, focused work.

A simple strategy to reduce time wastage

According to Parkinson's Law, a task will expand to fill the time available for its completion. So, if you have a report to write and you've blocked out half a day to write it, chances are it will take half a day.

Ashutosh Priyadarshy is the founder of Sunsama, software that helps users plan their day. Priyadarshy has thought a lot about Parkinson's Law and productivity. 'I think one of the most interesting applications I've seen for Parkinson's Law is to pick almost insanely small time periods for certain things and try to force your problem and solution into that space,' he explains.

In the early days of building Sunsama, Priyadarshy's team would often run two-day sprints to build new features. On the Monday morning, Priyadarshy would announce what he wanted to build and by Tuesday evening, the team would be ready to ship the new features to go live on the website. The team would then repeat the process on Wednesday and Thursday.

'In order to be able to achieve this, we had to figure out ways to take what we thought were really hard problems and break them down into things that could be done in two days.'

Perhaps surprisingly, forcing ourselves to work and think fast improves our mood. In one study, university students had to transcribe some recommendations on how the university could improve the course. These recommendations were presented to participants at a rate that was either marginally faster or considerably slower than an average reading speed. Students who were in the rapid presentation group were forced to read, think and work more quickly – and as a result, they reported feeling significantly happier than the second, slower group.

In my own life, I have experimented with using very small chunks of time to force myself to be ultra-productive. For example, I write regularly for various publications such as *Harvard Business Review*, Yahoo! Finance and the *Australian Financial Review*. I could easily spend several hours writing and polishing an article but instead, I timebox just one hour into my diary and force myself to produce a first draft within this period. I also have a physical clock on my desk, ticking down the minutes.

I have found that using an artificial time constraint gives me laser focus: it's like I am competing against the clock and I'm determined to win. And if you've ever played board games against me, you'll know that I am very competitive.

Some unusual research led by Echo Wen Wan from the University of Hong Kong suggests my 'compete against the clock' strategy is actually backed by science. Wan found that when a clock is visible and nearby, people tend to be able to maintain their energy across the day. Somehow, seeing the clock instils a sense of urgency, and this sense of urgency helps us maintain our motivation.

Priyadarshy explains that without the tight time constraint, it's easy to move through tasks passively and waste a lot of time. 'But when you're making that commitment to yourself, you're challenging yourself. And I think that effective and productive behaviour comes from setting what is basically like a goal to strive for.'

You would assume that to achieve extreme productivity in such small periods of time, Priyadarshy would have to block out all digital distractions. However, his approach has been to simply ignore them. 'Instead of focusing my energy on what I don't want to do, such as not checking Twitter or Slack, I try to just put all of my energy and focus on what I do want to do.'

Priyadarshy also shares with his colleagues what he plans to get done during the day to create some accountability. And the combination of time constraints and accountability naturally lead Priyadarshy to focus his time, energy and attention on the tasks he actually wants to do.

'I'm motivated to do what I said I was going to do. And so it's not like I don't check social media or Slack at all, because I do, but I'm able to just push them aside and get back to what I want to do, because I have that goal and that commitment both to myself and to the people I work with.'

Put it into action

1. Pick a task that you have to get done today, ideally something that would normally take you at least a couple of hours.
2. Challenge yourself to do the task in half the time it normally takes.
3. Block out this time in your diary using timeboxing.
4. If it helps, share your goal with other people for some extra accountability.

Nudge your way to better behaviour

My daughter is in the habit of taking about 356 soft toys to bed with her. (I'm obviously exaggerating – it's more like twenty: totally manageable). I'm currently trying to get her to change her behaviour to only taking one. But changing behaviour can be hard work. And not necessarily because behaviour change is hard, but because, often, we go about it in the wrong way.

It's easy to assume that changing deeply engrained behaviours requires us to make big changes or draw on all our willpower. But according to Nudge theory, making subtle changes to our environment can help to make big change almost effortless.

WordPress and Automattic co-founder Matt Mullenweg often thinks about small behavioural hacks he can make in his own life that will lead to the biggest payoffs. 'If what is closest to me in the bed when I wake up is the Kindle and not the phone, I'm more likely to read,' says Mullenweg. 'But if the phone is on top of the Kindle, I'm more likely to look at the phone. If I can reverse that order, it's a bit better. And I think it's good to look at every aspect of your life and say, "Okay, where's something that I can make it easy to do the thing that I want to do".'

The reverse is also true in Mullenweg's life. If he is trying to do deep, focused work and eliminate digital distractions, he turns his wi-fi off at the switch. Doing so makes it less tempting to get distracted online, because it would require him to stand up and walk over to his modem, switch it on and wait a minute or two for it to reconnect.

Research led by Paul Rozin from the University of Pennsylvania found support for Mullenweg's strategy, that small changes in where you place objects can lead to large changes in behaviour. In one study, Rozin and his colleagues varied the location of foods and serving utensils in a salad bar. They found that if a food was shifted 25 cm further away from the location in which patrons stand, people were about 10–15 per cent less inclined to choose this food. Similarly, if only a spoon rather than tongs was available, people were less inclined to choose foods that are easier to manoeuvre with tongs.

In his book *Work Rules*, former Senior Vice President of People Operations at Google, Laszlo Bock, described an experiment whereby he was trying to influence Googlers to make healthier food choices. In one scenario, healthy snacks were placed at eye level in transparent containers at the company's snacking stations. Unhealthy snacks were placed closer to the ground in opaque containers. This simple change led to a 30 per cent reduction in the number of calories consumed, and candy and fat consumption dropped by 40 per cent.

Consider what habits you are looking to change, and reflect on changes you can make to your environment to use your time more wisely. Look at all aspects of your life and ask yourself, 'What's something that I can change to make it easier to do the thing that I want to do, or harder to do the thing I don't want to do?'

I'll obviously be asking my daughter to read this chapter and design a soft toy restriction strategy as part of her Year 2 school work.

Put it into action

1. Think about a behaviour that you want to change. It might be something you want to do more of, or conversely, something you want to do less of.
2. If it's something you want to do more of, consider how you can redesign your environment to make it a tiny bit easier to

engage in the behaviour – just like Mullenweg did by leaving his Kindle on top of his phone.

3. If it's a behaviour you are trying to reduce, try to figure out what you can change in your environment to make it slightly harder to engage in the behaviour – just like Google did when putting unhealthy food in opaque containers close to the ground.

How to stop forgetting what you read

Most people have to read for work, some more than others. When it comes to reading non-fiction and work-related materials, I tend to be a binge reader. I'll have a month where I will read six or more books and a bunch of journal papers, and then the following month, it might just be one book of fiction. But during my binge-reading months, I often struggle to retain everything I want to remember from the books and papers I power through.

Scott Young, the bestselling author of *Ultralearning*, is obsessed with the process of learning and optimising it to work for him. One of the most important aspects about effective learning is retrieval. This is the process of your brain finding the information it has learned. The irony is that the place where we are introduced to the importance of retrieving information – school – doesn't actually teach us how to get better at it: accumulation is prioritised over retrieval, and sets us up for a lifetime of not being able to make the most of what we've learned. Clearly, this is highly inefficient.

One of Young's favourite studies into memory was conducted by Jeffrey Karpicke and Janell Blunt from Purdue University. The researchers divided participants into different groups and asked them to use different methods to study a text, knowing they would be asked questions about it later.

One group was asked to undertake repeated reviews, whereby they read the material over and over again until they felt they had learned it. Another group was asked to do free recall, whereby they read the text once, closed the book, and then tried to recall from memory everything that was covered.

But as with many great psychology studies, and Gillian Flynn novels, there was a twist (perhaps not as shocking as the one in *Gone Girl*, but a twist nonetheless). Before sitting the test, participants were asked how well they thought they learned the information. People who did repeat reviews gave themselves high marks, while those assigned free recall gave themselves poor marks. After all, trying to recall things from only reading a text once is pretty damn hard, right?

However, test results revealed the opposite. Those who practised free recall performed better on the test compared to those who did repeated reviews. So if you want to improve your ability to remember things, you need to practise remembering them, as opposed to merely looking at them.

For Young, this research changed how he approached reading. Like many of us, he read passively. Sure, he was highlighting and underlining passages in journal papers when researching his book *Ultralearning* and feeling productive in his reading, but he was struggling to recall specific things he had read.

'I recognised that if I want to be able to practise what I preach then I ought to be doing some retrieval practice,' explained Young. 'So I started the habit of just putting a few pages of loose leaf paper in the binder where I was storing the journal papers. And then when I was done with the paper, I tried to summarise it. I tried to recap what was in the paper, what were the findings, what were the things that I might use in the book.'

For Young, this made a huge difference as to how well he started to remember what he was reading. He also found he would approach the task of reading more actively, knowing that he had a free recall challenge awaiting him.

Put it into action

1. When you next set out to read an article or book, tell yourself that when you finish, you will have to write down everything you can remember.
2. Then, when you finish the text, open a blank document, or grab a sheet of paper and a pen, and write down a summary of what you have learned.
3. If there are elements that you feel are missing from your summary, feel free to return to the text. You can either write them straight into your summary or do a second free recall test where you include additional details from your second read.

How a mouse can give you productivity superpowers

If you spend a lot of your day sitting in front of a computer, your mouse probably gets quite the workout. You might use it to switch between screens or software, to highlight text, to copy and paste, or perhaps to scroll up and down a page. But what you might not have considered is how this unassuming little device is slowing you down.

Rahul Vohra is the founder and CEO of Superhuman, email software that claims to deliver the world's fastest email experience (and as a loyal Superhuman user, I can definitely vouch for this claim). Vohra is a designer and entrepreneur who spends much of his day at his computer. He thinks a lot about productivity, for both himself and for Superhuman. One of the ways he designed Superhuman to be such a speedy way to zoom through email comes down to the mouse.

'When I use Superhuman, I almost never touch the mouse,' Vohra told me. 'We designed Superhuman so you can do everything from the keyboard. You can fly through your inbox purely by typing. And that's a rule I abide by in almost every piece of software I use. I go above and beyond to make sure I'm learning those keyboard shortcuts and becoming more efficient and more productive as a result.'

He explained that when we rely on our mouse too much, we become slower at navigating around on our computer. Our brain has to get involved in the mechanical work of moving our elbow, wrist and fingers. And we do this almost unconsciously. Yet most of us wouldn't think twice about how much we use our mouse every day (I certainly didn't, prior to speaking to Vohra).

Vohra describes being able to 'play' Superhuman in the same way he can play the piano – through just using his fingers. 'And that creates a ton of efficiency'.

The key to reducing time spent with your mouse is not to feed it less cheese, but instead to invest time in learning keyboard shortcuts. This is something Vohra obsesses over. And if spending a Saturday night in learning new keyboard shortcuts isn't your idea of a good time, the good news is that most software shares a common set of shortcuts.

'Once you start to develop the muscle memory, you can very intuitively learn shortcuts in any new app that you pick up,' Vohra claims. For example, you probably know that Command or Control C and Command or Control V will let you copy and paste text or images. And Command or Control B/I/U will let you bold, italicise or underline text. These commands work across almost every software that you use. And fortunately, additional keyboard shortcuts you invest time in learning will also work across most software, which is great for productivity gains in whatever program you happen to be working in.

Put it into action

1. When working at your computer today, start to notice the actions for which you rely on your mouse most. For example, it might be clicking on the button to compose a new email, it might be scrolling up and down on webpages, or it might be opening and closing new windows.
2. Make a list of these common actions and research the keyboard shortcuts for doing each of them.
3. For two weeks, aim to learn one new keyboard shortcut per day. Repetition will help make it automatic, but if it's not sinking in and becoming habitual (i.e., you are still sometimes using your mouse to complete the action), don't move on to the next keyboard shortcut until the current one you are learning is locked into your muscle memory.

EFFICIENCY
A summary

Kill your zombies

Ask yourself: 'What are the projects I'm working on and the routine meetings I have that are not creating value?' For recurring meetings, ask yourself, 'Does it make sense for us to be meeting with this frequency? Or can this meeting be done just as well via email or asynchronous updates?'

Kill your zombies by eliminating these projects, activities and meetings.

The 30x rule

List all the activities you do more than thirty times per year and aim to outsource or automate them. Activities that are (or can be) rule-based are best for automation. Processes that are repetitive but do not always follow the exact same rules are more suited to outsourcing.

For automation, research software that can help with this. For outsourcing, there might be someone in your organisation – or alternatively, a virtual assistant – you could give tasks to.

Default to phone chats, not coffees

When you next receive a request for a coffee catch-up, reflect on whether you really want to say 'yes'. If you do genuinely want to help or meet with the other person, schedule a phone chat for a time that would otherwise be dead time, such as during your commute or a daily walk.

Delete all your meetings

Delete every meeting in your diary and accompany the deletion with a note to the organiser, providing them with three options. Option 1 is that they re-invite you to the meeting but specify the purpose of the meeting and the role they want you to play. Option 2 is that someone else can sub in for you and you don't have to attend. Option 3 is that you don't need to be at the meeting anymore, or better still, that the meeting doesn't even need to take place.

Discourage meeting attendance

Before booking a meeting and inviting other people, ask yourself 'Does every individual really need to attend?' Let meeting attendance be the decision of the attendee. Give people permission to decline meetings if they feel that they can't contribute or if attending the meeting doesn't contribute to achieving their goals.

Use videos instead of meetings

Before scheduling a meeting, think about whether it could be replaced with a video (or an email) update. Alternatively, think about the benefits of combining both: prepare a video that people can watch in their own time and then discuss it during the meeting.

Batch your meetings

Create rules for yourself for when you don't schedule or accept meetings. For example, if you are most cognitively sharp in the mornings, implement a 'no meetings' rule for several mornings per week.

If you have minimal control over your calendar, speak to the people who put meetings in your diary about the productivity gains that can come from batching meetings. Instead of having 'no meetings' blocks of time in your diary, try the reverse: have blocks of time during the week that are dedicated to meetings.

Mandate meeting pre-reads and make timely decisions

Ask team members to add items they want to discuss to a written agenda in a shared document the day before the meeting. All team members must read this document beforehand, and only allow comments from those in the meeting who have done so. If decisions are not made after five minutes of discussion, the leader should take responsibility for making any non-reversible decisions. Reversible decisions should be delegated to someone on the team. All decisions should be made prior to the next team meeting.

The To-Discuss list

Create a new list called To Discuss. You might even set up several To Discuss lists based on all the people you communicate with frequently.

Take out your To Discuss list when you are meeting with the person and work through everything on it. If you don't have a meeting scheduled, wait until you have a few items on your list before booking a meeting with them.

The three-label inbox solution

Create multiple inboxes in your email labelled To-Do, To-Do – Waiting, and Read. When you go into your inbox for the first time each day, sort all your emails into these three folders (or piles).

Pick a time of the day when you are feeling energetic to go through your To-Do pile. When you are feeling less energetic, go through your Read pile. Once every day or two, go through your To-Do – Waiting pile and see if you need to chase anything up.

Extreme timeboxing

Pick a task that you have to complete today, ideally something that would normally take at least a couple of hours. Challenge yourself to do the task in half the time it would normally require. Block out this time in your diary using timeboxing.

Change through nudges

Think about a behaviour that you want to change. If it's something you want to do more of, think about how you can re-design your environment to make it that tiny bit easier to engage in the behaviour. If it's a behaviour you are trying to reduce, think about what you can change in your environment to make it slightly harder to engage in the behaviour.

The free recall strategy

When you next finish reading an article or book, challenge yourself to write down everything you can remember. If there is information that you feel is missing from your summary, feel free to revisit the text. You can either write it straight into your summary or do a second free recall test where you include additional details from your second read.

Master keyboard shortcuts

When working at your computer, notice the actions for which you rely on your mouse most. Make a list of the common ones. Research the keyboard shortcuts for executing each of these actions. For two weeks, aim to learn one new keyboard shortcut per day.

FOCUS
Get into flow

I used to be a mobile phone addict. It was my crutch for any situation where I might be bored. I would pull out my smartphone when standing in line for a coffee. I would pull it out when having dinner with a friend and they left the table for a few minutes to go to the bathroom. It would be the first thing I would check when I woke up in the morning and the last when I went to bed at night. I would even check emails or scroll through Instagram when I brushed my teeth (in my defence, brushing one's teeth is pretty uneventful).

I behaved like this for many years. Thousands and thousands of hours were sunk into scrolling through my Instagram and Facebook feeds. Hours that I will never, ever be able to get back.

Research collated by MediaKix in 2016 suggests that around half of our daily phone time – nearly two hours – is spent on the top five social media platforms (Facebook, YouTube, Snapchat, Instagram and Twitter). Over the course of the year that translates to a staggering 30 full days. That is one whole month spent watching, reading, scrolling and clicking on things that probably are not significantly improving your life. In fact, it might be having the opposite effect. A review of studies published about mobile phone addiction suggests heavy usage is associated with a tonne of unfortunate outcomes, such as lower self-image and self-esteem, neuroticism, not to mention higher levels of anxiety and stress and poor sleep.

Mobile phone addiction is the archenemy of focus. In this section, we will delve into how the world's most successful people have managed to kick their digital addictions and how they get into flow and stay there.

You'll also learn why it's so important to work through the feelings of discomfort that come when we hit a stuck point. And we'll finish by helping you reframe how you think about procrastination.

Use behavioural architecture to transform your relationship with your phone

Adam Alter has spent a lot of time pondering his mobile phone usage. In fact, back in 2017, he wrote a book about it called *Irresistible*, which explores why so many people are addicted to digital devices. Alter is also a Professor of Marketing at New York University's Stern School of Business.

As someone who studies behaviour for a living, Alter thought he had his own relationship with his mobile phone under control. 'I thought I used my phone for an hour a day. I was actually using it between three and four hours,' he told me.

After discovering just how long he was spending on his phone every day, Alter reflected on why he might be using it so much and the occasions where usage was high. He realised that there was no period during the day when he couldn't reach his phone without moving his feet.

'Even when I was sleeping, the phone was by the bed. And during the day, it's either in my pocket or on the desk. It was always absolutely accessible at all times. And I realised that there were a lot of moments where as a sort of default, I would reach over, grab the phone, and then lose 10 minutes.'

Those 10 minutes add up over the course of a day. You only need to do that six times and bingo – you've lost an hour without even trying.

So Alter starting using behavioural architecture to redesign his relationship with phone. 'It's the idea that just as an architect might design a building or a city, you are the architect of your own environment, which then changes how you behave. And the things that are furthest away from you have less of an impact than the things that are close to you.'

Alter started to deliberately create physical distance between himself and his phone. He would only bring it close to himself when he had made a purposeful decision to do so. At home, Alter would keep his phone in a different room to the one he was currently in. In his office, Alter would lock his phone away in his filing cabinet.

Through making these simple changes, Alter's mobile phone usage dropped by 30 per cent.

Put it into action

1. Do an audit of your current mobile phone behaviour by looking at how much time you use it every day. Thankfully, technology companies have made that easy to do. On an iPhone, go to Settings and select Screen Time to find your data. On an Android device, go to Settings then Digital Wellbeing & Parental Controls to reveal your mobile phone usage.
2. Reflect on what is causing you to use your phone and the situations in which you are most likely to use it. Are there times of day when usage is high? Are there locations where you use it a lot? And in what types of situations are you most likely to reach for your phone?
3. Using behavioural architecture, think about how you can change your physical environment (such as where you store your phone during the day and night) to change your behaviour. Specifically, think about how your phone can be physically further away from you – in daytime and at night time – than it currently is.

Why you need a kSafe
for your phone

It's 9.30 am and you're working on a report. But you've hit a 'stuck' point and decide to relieve the feeling of stuckness by reaching for your phone and checking Instagram. Half an hour later, you emerge from your Instagram black hole and remember that you actually have a report to write.

Smartphone addiction is more common than we might think. Research has shown that the average person touches their phone 2617 times per day. That's a lot of swiping, typing, scrolling and clicking.

We often say to ourselves, 'I need to check my phone less'. But this strategy relies on pure willpower. And sadly, willpower is a limited resource. Perhaps it's time for an extreme strategy that physically restricts us from using our phone so that we don't have to tap into our willpower reserves.

Prior to becoming the CEO of Moment, a company that helps people use their phones in healthier ways, Tim Kendall was the President of Pinterest. During this time, he struggled a lot with his own phone usage. He started to research what he describes as 'brute force approaches' and discovered a product called the kSafe.

The kSafe is a lockable kitchen safe with a built-in timer. It was originally designed as a weight-loss aid in which dieters could lock away unhealthy food.

It's pretty hard to break a diet when all your chocolate is stashed in an unbreakable safe. But in recent years, the product has found a secondary purpose for those struggling with mobile phone addiction, as it's the perfect size to lock away smartphones.

Kendall initially tried experimenting with locking away his phone on weeknights, and then for a few hours on the weekend. While he doesn't use the kSafe regularly anymore, he found it effective at the time.

'The thing that works for me today is in my house, I have an office. And when I leave that office before I go and have dinner with my family, I just leave my phone in the office,' he explains. 'On my best nights, I don't go and get my phone until the next morning, which is effectively the same thing as putting it in a kitchen safe from 6 pm to 8 am.'

Put it into action

1. Search for 'kSafe' in Google and you will discover a plastic box with a built-in timer on the lid. Select the opaque, coloured box (out of sight, out of mind!) and decide what hours you want to restrict your phone usage. You might start small and lock your phone up for 30 or 60 minutes once a day. Try to build up to several hours to allow you to stay focused for longer chunks of time and gradually kick your mobile phone addiction.

2. If you happen to lead a team or a company, you could take things a step further. Perpetual Guardian founder Andrew Barnes, who pioneered the Four-day Week, created mobile phone lockers at the company's Auckland office. People who were not great at relying on discipline to stay off their phones found it helpful to lock their phone away in a locker for the day.

How a rubber band can tame digital addiction

We all know we should check our phone less, and certainly, turning off all notifications or putting our phone on Do Not Disturb can help reduce the amount of time we spend checking it. But Silicon Valley entrepreneur Kevin Rose found a more novel way to tame his mobile phone habits.

Rose has been named by *Time* magazine as one of the 25 Most Influential People on the Web and was an angel investor in companies including Facebook, Twitter and Square. A few years ago, he started to become increasingly aware of his mobile phone behaviour and realised he was picking up his phone more than 100 times per day. (Although considering the average person picks up their mobile phone over 200 times per day according to research Rose had read, 100 didn't seem all that bad.)

One method he experimented with was always putting his phone face-down on the table so it stopped flashing at him. But then he tried something a bit more unusual: he put a rubber band around the phone.

'When you see that rubber band, it just reminds you to pause for a second and you think to yourself, "Do I really need to pick up and use my device right now?" Oftentimes, the answer is no,' he told me.

Rose would position the rubber band so it would sit horizontally across the screen. The rubber band acts as a visual cue to stop the automatic behaviour of picking up his phone. 'Subconsciously, I didn't even realise I was doing it. But with the rubber band, I have

to deliberately move it out of the way if I want to use my device.' After all, Instagram doesn't look so good when there is a rubber band cutting through all the images.

Through applying this strategy, Rose reduced his daily pick-ups from more than 100 to around thirty. It forced him to be more deliberate when he checked his phone because there was literally a physical barrier that had to be removed. This proved to be enough to dissuade him from checking his phone unless it was actually important. And let's face it – there's no such thing as a TikTok emergency.

Put it into action

1. If you are looking to reduce the number of times you pick up your phone every day, find a rubber band and put it around your phone so it sits horizontally through the middle of your screen.
2. If you want to go ultra-hardcore on the rubber band strategy, find a second rubber band and position that vertically, so you have a rubber cross on your phone and will have to remove the rubber bands to use your phone.

Get your phone off the table to boost happiness

Think back to your last face-to-face meeting or coffee catch-up you had with a colleague or acquaintance. Aside from a notebook or laptop to take notes on, what else was sitting on the table? Chances are, your mobile phones. Although if you were meeting with Professor Elizabeth Dunn from the University of British Columbia's Psychology department, her phone would have been tucked away in her bag. (And she may well have shot you dagger eyes if she saw your phone on the table.)

'I got really curious about how smartphones were affecting social interactions when I noticed that these interactions were often punctuated by people looking down at their screens,' Dunn told me.

Dunn and her colleagues set up an experiment to subtly manipulate how much people were using their phones during a social interaction to understand what impact this had on the quality of the catch-up. To do this, Dunn took over a table in a local cafe for about eight months. Every night, Dunn and her colleagues invited a group of friends to come in and have dinner. The researchers paid for the dinner in exchange for the diners filling out surveys at the end of the meal (which sounds like the kind of study I would have liked to have been part of back in my university days).

Participants had no idea the research had anything to do with technology. One group were told to put their phones away during the meal, but it was simply framed among other housekeeping instructions. The second group were told they needed to have their phones out and available during the meal so that they could receive a brief survey via text halfway through. Sneaky.

After going through the housekeeping – and with phones either on or off the table – participants were able to just enjoy their meal and chat to their friends. At the end of the evening, participants completed a survey asking how much they enjoyed the night.

'What we saw was that people enjoyed this experience of dining out with friends significantly less when phones were out and available compared to when phones were put away,' Dunn explained.

It's easy to think that the simple act of having your phone on the table during a social interaction – whether that be a meeting, a coffee catch-up or a meal – has no impact. But having a screen right in front of us is a source of distraction and prevents us from being completely present.

Dunn has been a well-behaved academic psychologist and applied this research finding to her own life. 'I really do try when I'm out with my friends to put my phone away at dinner. And at home, we have pretty strict family norms about not having phones out.'

And when we can put our phones away and truly be present with those around us, we are most definitely using time wisely.

Put it into action

1. Keep your phone in your bag or out of sight when you are meeting with other people, whether it be for work or social reasons. It will help you stay more present, and more importantly, the social interaction will be far more enjoyable.

Make your
phone boring

Jake Knapp used to work as a product designer on Gmail. So not only does he know about all the forces on our smartphone that are competing for our attention, he actually helped design them. Yet despite understanding the mechanics of how mobile phone apps are designed to command our attention, he fell victim to it.

'Six years ago, I had this moment where I just realised, "I don't need that stuff on my phone,"' Knapp told me. Knapp's moment of clarity came when he was playing with his son. They were building train tracks. Knapp was looking at something on this phone and his son innocently asked, 'Dad, why are you looking at your phone?' His son didn't mean it in a judgemental way, he was simply curious. Which got Knapp thinking: Why *was* he looking at his phone?

Like most people, Knapp had felt guilty about the amount of time he spent on his phone. But he also started to feel angry about how much it was commanding his attention. So he decided to do something about it.

'I deleted Facebook, Instagram, YouTube, Twitter and Gmail from my phone. I even turned off Safari,' Knapp recalled.

What remained on Knapp's phone were the apps that had utilitarian value. 'I have podcasts, I have a camera, I have maps, I have music, I have a flashlight. I have all these things that are actually really amazing, but it's half of what most folks have on their iPhone. And for me, the distraction-free iPhone is super powerful. Because when I'm not sitting at a computer, then it's just me with just my thoughts. It's not this pull constantly to my pocket.'

Having a distraction-free phone had a huge impact on Knapp's ability to stay focused on big projects, such as writing his bestselling books *Sprint* and *Make Time*, as well as create Design Sprints at Google Ventures where he worked for several years.

So what does Knapp do in those times where so many of us instinctively pull out our phone, such as queueing for coffee? Is he dying a painful death from boredom?

'I do nothing. If I'm out for dinner and my friend goes to the bathroom, I'm just looking around the restaurant. I literally will just be bored for a minute. And I think being bored is pretty powerful. If you can have little pockets of boredom in the day, it lets your brain rest and, for me, it lets the subconscious come up with a solution to something, solve something, or propose an idea that I hadn't had before.'

Put it into action

1. Get out your phone and delete every single app that is hijacking your attention in an unhelpful way or that you go to in moments of boredom (social media, email, games and even

your internet browser). If that suggestion is sending your blood pressure through the roof, perhaps start with the app you find most addictive.

2. Check the apps that are left on your phone and ask yourself: Are they all utilitarian apps, that is, are they apps that solely serve a functional purpose in your life? If the answer is 'yes', you have successfully created a distraction-free phone.

3. Observe your behaviour and see how it changes now that you don't have a little distraction device in your pocket. And relish the moments of boredom, as you may accidentally become productive in them when your mind is allowed to wander.

A simple strategy to stop mindless scrolling

Have you ever been lazing on the couch at night and unconsciously picked up your phone? Yeah, me neither.

Okay, seriously, of course you have. You start scrolling through, looking at people's highlight reels, and getting seduced by the multitude of advertisements being served to you. Who knew how many essential gadgets, facial masks and vitamin-packed zero-calorie (yet mouth-wateringly delicious) protein balls you were missing from your life? I sure didn't.

Presumably, you finally stopped scrolling. But what led you to stop? Did your partner interrupt you? Did you feel hungry or thirsty? Were you sucked back into your Netflix binge? One thing I can guarantee is that you didn't stop because you got to the very end of the content on Instagram. It's the never-ending loop of social media that is one of the reasons why technology like this is so hard to step away from.

One way to fight back against being sucked into social media black holes is through stopping cues. Adam Alter, a Professor of Marketing at New York University's Stern School of Business and bestselling author of books on digital addiction, says stopping cues are one of the best ways to be more mindful about our digital behaviour. 'It's the idea that humans are like physical objects – we keep doing the same thing until some force acts on us to move us onto the next thing. And in the twentieth century, if you think about how we consumed media, there were a lot of these stopping cues built in.'

Alter gives the example of watching a TV show. Before the days of streaming and binging, you would watch one episode a week, which would typically last for between 30 and 60 minutes. At the end of an episode, you would be forced to stop and wait a week for the next episode. I know – I barely remember that feeling, either.

When reading a hardcopy newspaper, you reached the end of the paper and stopped. If you wanted to keep reading, you would have to wait for tomorrow's paper the following day. Likewise, getting to the end of a chapter in a book would signal for you to stop reading. And because of these inbuilt stopping cues, humans were really good at moving from one activity to the next.

Unfortunately, that all changed in the twenty-first century with the introduction of screen technology. Many of the companies that built the technology thought it might be a good idea to remove the stopping cues.

'The original version of Facebook actually had a button to click to show more content and you had to keep clicking that button. That seems like a trivial thing to have to do, but every time you clicked the button, you were making the decision to continue. But now, there's an infinite loop on pretty much any feed on any social network. That's true of email as well. Email is endless.'

But Alter says there is a simple solution to fight back against the lack of stopping cues – create your own. For example, you might select specific times of the day as a signal that it's time to turn off your phone.

For Alter, having dinner with his family is a stopping cue. The minute it's time for dinner, he will either switch his phone on flight mode or put it in another room. Likewise, he has certain hours at the weekend when his phone automatically goes on flight mode.

In my own life, one of my stopping cues is 90 minutes before bedtime. I automatically put my phone on the charger in my study, switch the lights off in the room, and don't go back in until the morning.

Put it into action

1. Think about introducing one or two stopping cues to reduce mindless usage of your phone (and other devices that you find problematic). Consider some of the daily rituals that you have in life, ideally ones that would be more enjoyable if you didn't have your phone. These might be mealtimes, winding down before bed or periods when you are doing focused work.

2. Create rules for yourself to make it clear when you stop using your phone. Follow them!

How to stop checking email on holiday

Founder and CEO of 1800-GOT-JUNK, Brian Scudamore, is a fan of 'going dark' while on holiday. This doesn't mean dressing up as an evil villain from a Marvel Comic, as I first envisaged when I heard this phrase. For Scudamore, going dark means being disconnected from email and being able to be fully present with his family, especially with his three young kids.

While going dark sounds good in theory, willpower, or a lack thereof, can often get in the way. 'It's so easy to be bored and be standing in a line somewhere and say "Uh, I'll have a quick glance at my email and see how things are doing,"' Scudamore admits. So instead, he put in place an extreme measure to avoid the need to use willpower in order to stay off email.

On Scudamore's last afternoon in the office before heading on holidays, his personal assistant changes the password to his email and social media accounts. He is literally locked out.

'I remember when my assistant first started changing my passcode. She'd say, "What if the office burns down?: I'm like, "Call 911. Call the fire department." What am I going to do if I'm off on vacation with my kids?'

Scudamore has never had anyone reach out and get in contact with him while on holiday. 'They trust that I trust them to do the job while I'm away. So I don't get on social media, I don't check in, and my brain is totally free from business. And I get to enjoy that family time and personal time. It could be a long weekend of four days. It could be a three-week stint. I think my longest is about six weeks being com-pletely disconnected from the company.'

For Scudamore, he prefers to be 100 per cent focused on his business or 100 per cent out. 'There's so much intensity of pace that I've got to protect and look out for my own mental health.'

Put it into action

1. Think about which digital communication channels you find most distracting. This might be email, Slack (or another messaging platform), social media or something else entirely.
2. If you are not lucky enough to have a personal assistant, ask a friend to change your password before you go on holidays or whenever you want to 'go dark'. Make sure your friend writes down the new password somewhere!
3. If this sounds too extreme, consider using website- and app-blocking software such as Freedom.to, which you can program to lock you out of any software application or website during times of day that you specify.

Give yourself
more solitude

Think back to the last time you were on your own either going for a walk, standing in a queue or commuting on public transport. To prevent that horrible feeling of boredom, you might have taken out your phone to consume some form of content. Perhaps you listened to a podcast or flicked through social media. Or maybe dipped into your inbox.

If you spend most of your solo waking hours (when you are not actually working) staring at a screen or consuming content, you are subjecting yourself to solitude deprivation. Solitude deprivation is a state where you're never alone with your own thoughts.

The term solitude deprivation was coined by Professor Cal Newport in his widely acclaimed book *Digital Minimalism*. Perhaps not surprisingly, it's a state that leads to an increase in anxiety and a reduction in professional insights or breakthroughs.

To avoid it, Newport recommends undertaking one or two activities every day without your phone. 'It might be as simple as doing something around the house each day where there's no earbuds and no phone. Something as simple as that can have a major impact on your cognitive health, anxiety levels and happiness,' explains Newport.

When I first learned about solitude deprivation, I could immediately relate. When I wasn't working or spending time with other people, I was constantly consuming some type of input, normally in the form of podcasts. I had convinced myself that this was a good thing – I was learning something new, right? And don't we need to be constantly 'achieving' something with our time to optimise our productivity?

After reading *Digital Minimalism*, I started an experiment. I looked at the two main occasions on which I was consuming podcasts. The first was during the five hours I spent exercising every week (podcasts help me block out the pain!), and the second was my daily commute into the office, a 40-minute-long journey each way (pre-COVID times, of course).

I challenged myself to reduce 'input' time by 50 per cent. I would allow myself to listen to podcasts or other inputs for half of my commute time and half of my gym time. And for the other 50 per cent, I would consume nothing.

The results were immediate and striking. I felt my creativity sky-rocket and I was bombarded with insights and ideas during my quiet time. It was as if my brain was so relieved to be given space to ponder and produce. I was also struck by the fact that I was literally the only person in my vicinity who was engaging in this bizarre experiment – which if I'm honest, made me feel rather smug.

Newport incorporates significant amounts of phone-free (and thus input-free) time into his day. 'I do walks and exercise without my phone. When I'm at home, my phone will typically be in my bag. I don't accept the premise that I'm like an emergency room doctor that needs to be accessible at all times on a communication device. And once you change your mindset to one where it's like, "I use my phone to do various things but it's not something I always have with me," you just naturally get lots of solitude.'

For Newport, instead of stimulus consumption being a default activity, it has instead become something he schedules. 'I ask myself, "When am I going to get input? What input is it going to be?" So if I know, for example, I have a lot of yard work to do, I might say, "Great, I'm going to listen to this particular podcast."'

'It's not that there's a hard and fast rule, but I plan when I'm going to do stimuli. I ask myself, "Do I want the silence, or is this a good chance to listen to something?" If you think of the phone as a tool you occasionally use, not a constant companion, it can really make a big difference in terms of getting more solitude.'

Put it into action

1. Reflect on the common occasions that you are on your own and consuming content via your phone, such as social media, podcasts, games, news or audio books.
2. Set yourself a goal of reducing consumption time to avoid solitude deprivation. For example, my aim was to halve the time I spent consuming content to free up several hours to experience solitude.
3. Put your plan into action and make it easier for yourself by putting your phone out of reach during these times. And when the time arrives, simply let yourself be with your own thoughts.

How to use your physical environment to get into flow

When Google's Executive Productivity Advisor Laura Mae Martin was growing up, her dad often used to work from home (such a trailblazer!). She noticed he would go into his home office to work and then he would come out at the end of the day when he was done.

'We knew we were never allowed to bother him when he was in his office and he told me that originally, he only worked from that room because that's where his desktop computer and ethernet connection was. He didn't have a laptop when he first started working from home.'

Martin advises people to pretend they are like her dad – that is, imagine you have a desktop computer and ethernet connection somewhere in your home and make that your work spot. Doing so helps your brain with state-dependent recall, which means every time you go to that location, the same sights, sounds and smells you associate with working are there and it makes it easier to get into flow. 'If you're switching spots every day, it's harder for your brain to get into that space of saying, "This is where I work,"' explains Martin.

Being deliberate about where to work from is something Georgetown University Professor and author of *Deep Work*, Cal Newport, has pondered. He deliberately links different locations with different types of tasks.

'When I'm trying to solve a theoretical computer science proof, the rituals I use almost always involve various walking routes around my town,' explains Newport. But when he's doing writing work, you'll find Newport approaching it in a completely different way.

'In my house, I had a custom library table built that was reminiscent of the tables at the university library where I used to work as an undergraduate, with brass library lamps next to the dark wood bookcases. And I have a ritual for writing where I clear off that whole desk and I just have a bright light shining right down on the desk and it's just me and my computer.'

Martin gives another piece of advice about your physical environment to those working from home: make sure you have areas in your home where you never do work. 'This helps create mental boundaries because if you're inviting work into your home, you want somewhere like your bedroom or the living room where you never have work.'

Martin suggests thinking about work like a guest in your house. 'If you had a guest who was staying for a really long time, you wouldn't say, "Hey, just come into my bedroom anytime you want." You would give them a separate space and you would have boundaries.'

Put it into action

1. Think about the main categories of work that you do. For example, your work buckets might fall into: shallow work, such as email; deep work, such as strategic thinking or writing; phone calls; video meetings, and so on.
2. Consider what sort of location-based rituals you will link to each type of activity.
3. After a few weeks of practising these rituals, you should find that getting into flow becomes far easier and quicker because your brain associates the location-based cues with certain types of work.
4. Finally, think about the places in your home that are no-go zones for work and that are purely about relaxation and non-work activities.

How a second computer will help you stay on task

If you're like most people, you probably have just one computer. It's probably a laptop, given so many people split their work between an office and their home nowadays. That makes Dr Catriona Wallace – founder of fintech and ASX-listed company Flamingo AI, founder of Ethical AI Advisory and chair of Boab AI – unusual in that she has several computers. And not just because she has an extreme love of technology and happens to be one of the world's most cited experts on the topic of artificial intelligence and bot strategy.

Like most people, Wallace started off with just one machine that she would use for everything: email, entertainment, research and creative work. 'I was finding that when all my tasks were done on the same computer, it was easy to get distracted,' explains Wallace.

So she tried an experiment. She sourced three additional laptops from her office and home. And she allocated each one a job, based on the main types of tasks she does for work.

'One of the laptops is my email machine. Another is for creative work, such as designing presentations, marketing stuff and making videos. The third machine is for doing research. And another machine is purely for entertainment. I use it when I want to have a break and watch Netflix or some crazy things my family has sent me.'

Wallace finds this strategy makes it far easier to focus. 'In the same way that if you are sitting with a human, you are focused on what that person is saying, I find the same is true for my laptop strategy. If I am with my email laptop, I am 100 per cent focused on just doing email, in the same way I would be focused on a task if I was working on it with a real human. I find there is an emotional attachment to the machine that does the particular function, as well as a mental attachment. So I am super productive and focused because that's all this machine does with me.'

Put it into action

1. Now, the obvious disclaimer to this strategy is that it does require a fair amount of privilege, as not everyone can afford to buy more than one computer (hell, not everyone can afford even one computer). However, here is the most cost-effective way to apply this strategy: start by using it to delineate between deep work and shallow work. Shallow work typically only requires email software and messaging software, both of which demand minimal computer power. Therefore, your additional laptop investment can be a low-cost, basic model, which can be bought for around $200, or even less if it's second-hand.

2. Treat the low-cost laptop as your shallow workstation and use it for all email communication and instant messenger communication. You might even have a specific physical location in your home or office for it.

3. Use your main computer for deep work tasks. Given it is your main computer, and probably a significantly better machine, it will help to create positive associations with this type of work – arguably the more important and value-adding parts of your job that you engage in.

4. If you do have funds to invest in additional laptops, you could further delineate the types of work you do, as Wallace did. You could have a third machine that is just for creative work or other categories of work, and a fourth one solely for entertainment.

A simple trick
to get unstuck

Guardian columnist and author Oliver Burkeman describes himself as a recovering perfectionist. 'I'm always at pains to say this because there's a really annoying thing about perfectionism – people use it to be self-critical but secretly, they are boosting themselves up,' he says.

It reminds him of the way people are meant to answer the question, 'What are your greatest flaws?' in a job interview. 'Oh, I'm just too conscientious about my perfect output,' jokes Burkeman.

But for Burkeman, his perfectionistic tendencies impeded his ability to work. 'It screwed me up for a long time. It is relentless and it just makes it impossible to enjoy doing any of the work.'

Burkeman's perfectionism led to him having big struggles with writer's block. He constantly worried that what he was writing was not going to be good enough. Other people had given him the advice to just write and let his inner editor go to sleep for a while. But it didn't help. 'You actually want what you write to be good.'

But then Burkeman heard about a strategy used by other writers who had shared his struggle. The strategy involves typing out a rough draft of what he is working on. He then prints it out. And then he types it back onto the computer.

This somewhat bizarre process tricks Burkeman into getting into a flow state as it shifts him into editor mode. 'What's happening when I'm typing it in again is that I'm making all sorts of changes. But I'm making them almost unconsciously in the same way that on a good writing day, you're almost not conscious of the words flowing out. And you're not doing that very conscious kind of edit.

'Obviously, a book has to have that phase of editing as well when you're very consciously inspecting every word. But I find that it's a wonderful compromise because when you're typing it in again, you don't have to start from a blank page. So you're not worried about dredging it out of your soul in some sort of terribly melodramatic and stressful fashion.'

Put it into action

1. If you are experiencing writer's block – that is, you are struggling to make a start on your work, whether it be a report, writing code or creating a presentation, for example – try to create a really average first draft. Avoid self-censorship and just 'write'.
2. When you have finished the draft, print it out.
3. Type it back into your computer and experience yourself hopefully getting into flow and reducing your self-censorship.

How a script can help you come unstuck

While writing this book, I hit many 'stuck' points. I frequently found myself working on a chapter and feeling as if I couldn't push away at it anymore. I needed a break. And my instinct was to relieve myself with a digital distraction such as checking my phone or email. Or making a snack. Or mopping the floor. (Kidding. I really hate mopping.)

Professor of Marketing, Adam Alter, experiences stuck points frequently. But instead of automatically reaching for his phone, he does something else. 'The best thing you can do is to have a script that you follow in those moments, especially if you find that it's a regular thing for you that you hit these points where your default would be to check the phone.'

As an example, Alter suggests that your script could be that every time you hit one of those moments, you're going to go for a two-minute walk. 'I often do this. I walk around the floor in my office building. And at home, I'll just take a stroll outside or I'll walk upstairs from my office, which is in the basement.'

He also has a treadmill desk in his office for such an occasion. This short walk acts as a natural resetting mechanism. And after taking the brief walk, he can sit back down and pick back up again with his work.

The other way Alter overcomes stuck points is to reflect on the things that he wished he had more time to do, and then doing them when he reaches a stuck point. For example, there is always new research being published that Alter, as a researcher, need to be across. He is frequently sent the tables of contents for academic journals, but felt that he never had time to go through them properly. So another script that Alter created for himself was that when he feels stuck, he will take some time out to read the tables of contents.

'In those moments when I'm really stuck, I'll devote maybe an hour to going through those tables of contents and reading the papers that really stick out and seem interesting. And so I'm turning that period of being stuck into something that's much more useful that I otherwise wouldn't have time to do.

'Whenever I hit the wall on the primary stuff, such as writing a paper, I can turn to the secondary stuff and it's time spent wisely, rather than time squandered.'

Put it into action

1. To create your stuck script, think about two categories of activities that you could turn to when you hit the wall. The first category should be quick activities, such as going for a brief walk, that you can do when you don't have time for a longer break from your main task. The second category of activities should be what Alter refers to as 'secondary activities' – something that is beneficial for your work and requires a decent amount of time, but is not the primary task you are working on. For example, it might be reading some articles or reaching out to some networks.

2. Write down your scripts and pin them to your computer or somewhere in your office. They should say something like, 'When I feel stuck, I will go for a two-minute walk.' Or 'When I feel stuck, I will catch up on reading some industry publications'.

3. After following these scripts for a while, they should start to become habitual. You might also want to try varying your scripts and experimenting with different activities. Remember: you want to make the activities enjoyable ones, otherwise, it's going to be too tempting to drift back into old habits and reach for your phone.

Why you need to use a Struggle Timer

Many productivity experts believe that our ability to focus is like a muscle that needs training. The more deep, focused work we do, the stronger our muscle will become and the easier we will find it to engage in deep work. But Scott Young, critically acclaimed author of *Ultralearning*, sees things differently. He believes that our ability to focus is about managing one's emotions.

Making progress on big, important projects is often frustrating, involves getting negative feedback and, at times, questioning your abilities (which, for me, brings back memories I had tried to repress of writing an 80,000-word PhD thesis). These challenges can create an instinctual aversion to getting started and then maintaining focus.

Young has tried several strategies to improve his capacity to stay focused. One such strategy is called the Struggle Timer. The idea for the Struggle Timer emerged when he was contemplating his approach to studying and learning new material. One of his many accomplishments is that he learned the entire MIT computer science curriculum – which normally takes four years – in less than twelve months. And he did this without taking any classes.

When he was working on solving a problem during the course, he would often wonder: How quickly should he look at the answer when he couldn't identify the right one? 'The approach that I took during the MIT challenge is that you should get the right answer immediately. So as soon as you get stuck, you should look at the right answer because immediate feedback is important.'

Over the years, Young shifted his view and now believes it often makes sense to struggle a little bit on harder problems for two reasons. Firstly, you can sometimes solve the problem with a bit more time, and therefore struggling for a little bit longer can be beneficial because you might need that time to get to the right answer. And working on getting to the right answer yourself is much more valuable than just looking it up.

Secondly, Young believes there's benefit to struggling for a little longer because it allows you to appreciate the right answer better. 'Because of that negative emotional state, the feeling of frustration when you do encounter the answer will be much more memorable because it will have solved a problem that you were like, "Ah, that's how you solve it!" as opposed to, "Oh yeah, I guess that makes sense."'

Young took these insights and now, when he feels himself struggling with a problem or a task, he sets the Struggle Timer for five or ten minutes. And often, this additional five or ten minutes can make the difference between solving a problem or getting back into flow – and giving up or procrastinating on another task.

Put it into action

1. When you feel like you have hit a stuck point on a task, set a timer for five to ten minutes. Often, that is all it takes to push through the negative emotions you are feeling and get over the obstacle you are experiencing. (You might even wish to purchase a five- or ten-minute hourglass timer and literally label it Struggle Timer, as labelling emotions can lessen their intensity.)
2. If you are still struggling after ten minutes, give yourself permission to take a break. But chances are, you'll be back in

flow and the negative emotions will have passed. And if you use the Struggle Timer in the context of solving a problem, the extra few minutes may well have been enough time to get to the answer.

How getting comfortable with discomfort will make you more productive

We all have work we need to do that feels just plain hard. It's the kind of work where we are looking for any excuse to be pulled away – and predominantly by digital distractions. When you reach a stuck point on preparing a sales presentation, the easiest thing to do is check your Instagram feed or hop on over to YouTube. As humans, we are pretty bad at sitting with discomfort, so digital distractions are an effective way to quickly diminish these feelings. But of course, in the long-term, such behaviour is not helping us get our work done.

Behavioural design expert and author of the hugely popular books *Hooked* and *Indistractable*, Nir Eyal, recognised this happening in his own life. He has always found writing really hard work. 'It's never been effortless. It takes a lot of time and a lot of concentration. I feel all sorts of negative emotions such as boredom, uncertainty, fear and fatigue when I write.'

Eyal refers to these emotions as internal triggers, which lead him to want to distract himself from the task at hand. 'So in the middle of writing, I'll get this idea, "Oh, I should probably check email real quick". Because that's productive, that's a kind of work, isn't it?'

But, of course, he knows this is not work; it's the opposite – it's a distraction. It wasn't what he had planned to do with his time, which was write.

One strategy he uses to avoid succumbing to distractions is called Surfing the Urge. Surfing the Urge involves first noticing the sensation you are feeling, such as boredom or anxiety. Eyal then labels the sensation. 'I'm feeling anxious right now.' 'I'm feeling fearful that this essay is not going to be any good.' 'This is boring.' Whatever the sensation might be, he writes that sensation down.

'It's incredibly empowering to write down what you felt and to not explore it with contempt. A lot of people will jump to beating themselves up. They will say things like "I have an addictive personality," or, "I have a short attention span," or whatever the case might be. Instead, what we want to do is to explore it with curiosity, not contempt.'

Like a surfer balancing on a surfboard, Eyal rides emotions as if they are waves. They rise, they crest, and then they subside. And if we can allow ourselves to be curious about that sensation, as opposed to trying to resist it with abstinence (which can actually make the problem worse), whatever unpleasant sensation we are feeling will eventually subside and wash over us.

Scientists have found that the simple act of labelling our emotions reduces their intensity. In one fascinating study, arachnophobic participants were asked to stand near a tarantula that was locked in a transparent container (one of the less desirable research studies for a university student to participate in, no doubt). Half the participants were asked to label the sensations and emotions they were experiencing, while the other half were told to distract themselves or apply other strategies that might help reduce their anxiety.

One week later, everyone was brought back to the lab and asked to stand next to the spider again. Those who labelled their sensations and emotions were significantly less scared of the black furry creature, demonstrating that simply labelling our emotions helps them fade away.

Put it into action

1. When you are trying to do deep, focused work but you are feeling an unpleasant sensation, instead of succumbing to the urge to release yourself from it through checking social

media or engaging in another form of distraction, take a moment to label the sensation. Acknowledge to yourself how you are feeling and write it down.

2. Remind yourself that, like a wave, sensations are transient, and it will crest and subside.

3. Consider setting yourself a goal and say that you will keep pushing through the sensation for the next ten minutes (you might even want to use Young's Struggle Timer idea – see page 162), and if it hasn't subsided, you will let yourself check TikTok. But what you will probably find is that after ten minutes, the sensation will have passed, and you will have successfully avoided letting yourself be distracted.

How to use music to get into flow

It's 9 am and time to start your workday. You have a pile of challenging work to get through but your local news website is looking much more interesting than crunching data in an Excel spreadsheet. An hour later, you emerge glassy-eyed from the internet rabbit hole you ended up travelling down. And surprisingly, the data hasn't crunched itself. Data is like that, though.

And as you know, when you have hard work to do, it can be hard to get started, let alone get into flow.

Wired magazine co-founder Kevin Kelly has experienced that feeling many times, especially when it comes to writing. 'I'm a born editor, but not a born writer,' Kelly admits. 'When I have some really hard writing to do, that first draft is a killer for me. I write in order to find out what I think, because I don't know what I think until I write it, and then as I begin to write it, I realise I don't have any idea what I'm talking about.'

Kelly uses a very specific strategy to get through writing the tough first draft. 'I have a song that I play on a loop, with headsets, and it just goes round and around and around. It's the same song and there's something weird about the experience of listening to it on repeat. It's very soothing. Just hearing the song makes me productive. Distractions flow away and it's kind of like being in a work trance.'

Kelly likens his technique to people who work in cafes because the background noise helps them focus. And indeed, several guests on *How I Work* have shared a similar strategy.

WordPress co-founder Matt Mullenweg has specific playlists he will work to. 'I like deep house focus playlists because there's no words or very few words and they have a nice beat behind it. But if I really need to get in the zone, my general thing is just picking a single song and having that on repeat. And that can be really anything so long as it's a song that I like so it's pleasurable to listen to. Your mind backgrounds it after the first or second listen and I've just found that to be a really effective technique.'

Mullenweg's go-to song when I interviewed him on my podcast was Drake's 'Nice for What'. Kelly has listened to the same song for years: a Bulgarian men's choir singing a Gregorian chant.

According to researchers, listening to a song on repeat can help us get into a flow-like state. In one study published in the *Psychology of Sport and Exercise* journal, netball players were asked to select music that made them feel absorbed and captivated – in other words, in a state of flow. A variety of songs were chosen by the netballers, ranging from Massive Attack's 'Unfinished Symphony' to 'Two Tribes', a song released by Frankie Goes to Hollywood in 1984. The netball players were then asked to shoot goals. When they heard their preferred music playing in the background, their shots were more accurate. The music that elicited flow enhanced their performance.

Put it into action

1. Pick a song or playlist that you like listening to. Anecdotally, music with fewer lyrics (or no lyrics) tends to work more effectively. (Having said that, I went through a stage of listening to 'Yorktown' from *Hamilton* while I worked, which probably has about 5,697 words in the lyrics.)
2. Play the music on repeat while you are doing work that requires focus and being in a state of flow for a few work sessions.
3. After doing this several times, your brain will start to associate the music with a flow state and you'll start to find it easier to switch into flow through simply turning on your music.

An unconventional way to achieve creative flow

If you have ever binge-watched Netflix, fallen in love with a character from your favourite TV show or been moved to tears or laughter by something you watched on the box, chances are, the concepts that grabbed or moved you were born in a writers' room.

A writers' room is a place where story ideas are uncovered, characters are created and fleshed out, and ultimately, decisions are made on which direction to take a show. Needless to say, they are places where creativity is critical.

Award-winning screenwriter Glen Dolman, who created supernatural drama *Bloom*, among many other shows, has a very specific vibe he tries to foster in a writers' room. 'I try to create a space where people can be creative and open, fun and free, and even quite silly. The stories I like to tell are emotional and raw and I need the writers to feel really comfortable with each other.'

Dolman recounted a story he heard about Richard Curtis, whose writing credits include *Four Weddings and a Funeral* and *Notting Hill*. 'He talked about the ideal environment for a writers' room as being that stage at the end of a dinner party, when everyone's had a few drinks and everyone's funny. That's the headspace you've got to get into at 8 am when you all get to work.'

For Dolman, he found one of the most effective ways to get into that headspace is to overshare and be extremely vulnerable. While it might feel uncomfortable, a surprising overshare jolts people out of autopilot and starts to open people up to matching the vulnerability.

As well as the obvious benefits of vulnerability leading to a greater sense of safety amongst a team, the surprise factor that comes with an overshare yields creative benefits.

A study published in *Leadership Quarterly* examined how leaders could boost creativity within a team. The researchers had leaders run a one-hour problem-solving session with small groups of people. In one group, leaders were asked to behave in a conventional manner. But in the experimental group, leaders were asked to behave in novel or unconventional ways. For example, they spelled out their name for the group in colourful plastic magnetic letters; they delivered the instructions for the task at hand on the back of T-shirts that team members were instructed to wear; and the leader stood on the table to deliver feedback to people as they worked through the task. The leaders also had participants write down their ideas on socks, which were then hung up on a clothesline.

The researchers found that a leader's unconventional behaviour not only increased creativity but also led to people experiencing a stronger attachment to each other. A shared unconventional experience increases comfort and honesty, which in turn enhances creativity.

Put it into action

1. If you are assembling a group for creative thinking, such as for a brainstorm, think about some unconventional approaches you could take throughout the session.

2. Consider how you might kick off the session with something surprising, such as an overshare (like Dolman does) or providing instructions about the session in a novel way (such as on the back of T-shirts like the leaders in the experiment did).

3. Think about what additional unconventional behaviours or events could take place throughout the session to continue to boost cohesion and creativity among the group. For example, you might ask people to dress up in strange costumes halfway through a workshop or ask people to give themselves amusing nicknames. (Or you might think my suggestions are completely silly and come up with your own better ones.)

The real reason
you're procrastinating

Even though Tim Herrera used to edit the Smarter Living section for the *New York Times*, which covers how to build better habits for work and life, Herrera is a procrastinator.

'For my entire life, I've been a habitual procrastinator. I'm notorious for it,' he admits. But after editing a piece on procrastination by Charlotte Lieberman, Herrera started to think differently.

'I think it's easy to write off procrastination by saying "I just didn't feel like it", or "I was distracted", or "I saw a tweet that sent me into a Wikipedia wormhole". But at its root, procrastination isn't about putting off a specific task. It's associated a lot more with the emotions that we're having regarding that task.'

He learned that if, for example, he was avoiding writing and was instead wasting time on Twitter, it wasn't because he was lazy. It was because he was feeling anxiety about the piece he was writing. So instead of seeing procrastination as simply being about putting off doing a task, it's actually about wrestling with the emotions that you have associated with the task.

This realisation was an a-ha moment for Herrera. 'The story helped me reframe the way that I viewed procrastination, and my old view was preventing me from doing certain things. Being aware of all the factors that go into why we're procrastinating was really powerful.'

Herrera realised that, at its core, procrastination was about managing his negative feelings around a task, such as anxiety, as opposed to him just being poor at managing his time. He also learned that the *way* he was procrastinating – checking Twitter – was exacerbating the problem. Through the provision of numerous likes and follows and interesting bits of information, Twitter gave Herrera many a dopamine hit, thus rewarding him for choosing to procrastinate.

Through understanding that procrastination was an emotion-management problem as opposed to a time-management one, Herrera started to implement strategies to help him manage his emotional state and by doing so, stay on task. One method that worked for him was making himself accountable to another person, so that if he missed a deadline, it would negatively impact that person.

'Making someone else unhappy, as opposed to finishing an article, is the thing that gives me most anxiety. And so, instead of thinking, "I will do anything to put off writing the story because I just don't want to do it," it becomes a matter of, "I will do anything to make sure I don't mess up this person's day, so I need to do this story".'

Herrera also tried to incorporate structures and habits into his day, so that at a certain time of day, he does his writing. And at another time of day, he edits. 'Trying to build habits around these things is such a powerful tool because it takes away the idea of self-control or willpower. You're just not thinking about it, you're just doing it.' And by making it automatic, it takes the emotions out of the task at hand.

Put it into action

1. The next time you find yourself procrastinating, stop beating yourself up about it or labelling yourself as lazy or unproductive. You're just human. Research led by Michael Wohl found that forgiving yourself for procrastinating leads to doing it less in the future.
2. Reflect on your feelings towards the task you are avoiding. A large part of overcoming procrastination is learning how to manage a negative emotional state, such as feeling anxious about a certain task.

3. Try to understand why you are experiencing negative emotions in relation to the task and consider how you could make it a more positive experience. You could look at reframing your motivation, like Herrera did. Habitualising tasks that you find yourself deferring can also help to take the emotion out of them.

FOCUS
A summary

Use behavioural architecture to overcome digital addiction

Audit your mobile phone behaviour by looking at how much time you use it every day. Reflect on what is causing you to use your phone and the situations you are most likely to use it in. Think about time of day, location and situations where you are most likely to reach for your phone.

Using behavioural architecture, think about how you can change your physical environment (i.e. where your phone physically lives) to modify your behaviour. Specifically, think about how your phone can be physically further away from you during the day and night than it currently is.

Lock your phone in a kSafe

Buy a kSafe – a plastic box with a built-in timer in the lid. Select the opaque box and decide what hours you want to restrict your phone usage. Then lock your phone up! If you happen to lead a team or a company, you could take things a step further and give staff the option to lock their phones away during meetings or parts of their workday.

Put a rubber band around your phone

Find a rubber band and put it around your phone so it sits horizontally through the middle of your screen. Take things to the next level by positioning a second rubber band vertically, so you have a rubber cross on your phone, meaning you will have to remove the rubber bands whenever you want to use it.

Leave your phone in your bag

Keep your phone in your bag or out of sight when you are meeting with other people – whether that's for work or social reasons. It will help you stay more present, so you'll be able to participate more effectively in the conversation, but more importantly, the interaction will be far more enjoyable.

Create a distraction-free phone

Delete every single app on your phone that is hijacking your attention or that you use in moments of boredom. Check the apps that are left on your phone and ask yourself: Are they all utilitarian apps? If the answer is yes, you have successfully created a distraction-free phone.

Use stopping cues to stop scrolling

Introduce one or two stopping cues to reduce mindless usage of your phone. Daily rituals can be great stopping cues – ideally rituals that would be more enjoyable if you didn't have your phone. These might be mealtimes, time before bed or periods when you are doing focused work. Create rules for yourself to make it clear when you stop using your phone, such as, 'I stop using my phone during mealtimes'.

Lock yourself out of email

Think about which digital communication channels you find most distracting. Ask a friend to change your password before you go on holidays or whenever you want to 'go dark'. Make sure your friend writes down the new password somewhere.

Overcome solitude deprivation

Reflect on the common occasions that you are on your own and consuming content via your phone – anything from social media, podcasts and games to news or audio books. Set yourself a goal of reducing consumption time to avoid solitude deprivation, because we all need time to be alone with our thoughts. Put your plan into action – and make it easier for yourself by putting your phone out of reach during these times. When the occasion arises, simply let yourself be with your own thoughts.

Create location-based rituals

Think about the main categories of work in your role and start to create location-based rituals for them. Consider what sort of physical environment you ideally want to inhabit for each type of work and design rituals that will suit best. After a few weeks of practising them, you should find that getting into flow becomes far easier and quicker because your brain associates the location-based cues with certain kinds of work.

Have different computers for different types of work

Invest in a second laptop or computer. Treat the lower cost laptop as your shallow work workstation and use it for all email communication and instant messenger communication. Use your main computer for deep work tasks.

Re-type your first draft

If you are battling writer's block – say, you are struggling to make a start on your work, whether it be a report, writing code or creating a presentation – create a really average first draft. When you have finished the draft, print it out. Type it back into your computer and edit as you go, to experience yourself hopefully getting into flow and reducing your self-censorship.

The Stuck Script

To create your stuck script, think about two categories of activities that you could insert into your script. The first category should be quick activities, such as going for a brief walk, that you can do when you don't have time for a longer break. The second category of activities are secondary activities – activities that are beneficial for your work and require a decent amount of time but are not the primary task you are working on.

Write down your scripts and pin them to your computer. Examples include, 'When I feel stuck, I will go for a two-minute walk' and 'When I feel stuck, I will catch up on reading some industry publications'.

After following these scripts for a while, they should start to become habitual.

The Struggle Timer

When you feel like you have hit a stuck point on a task, set a timer for five to ten minutes. Often, that is all it takes to push through the negative emotions you are feeling and get over the obstacle you are experiencing. If you are still struggling after ten minutes, give yourself permission to take a break.

Surf the urge

When you are trying to do deep, focused work but you are feeling an unpleasant sensation, instead of succumbing to the urge to release yourself from it by going to grab a snack or resorting to another form of distraction, take a moment to label the sensation. Acknowledge to yourself how you are feeling and write it down. Remind yourself that, like a wave, sensations are transient, and they will pass.

Consider setting yourself a goal to push through the sensation for the next ten minutes, that is, surf the urge, and if it hasn't subsided, you will let yourself check your Instagram feed (or whatever else). But what you will probably find is that after ten minutes, the sensation will have passed.

Listen to a track on repeat

Pick a song or playlist that you like listening to. Play the music on repeat while you are doing work that requires focus and being in a state of flow. After repeating this several times, your brain will start to associate the music with a flow state, and you'll start to find it easier to switch into flow by simply turning on your music.

Overshare to get creative

If you are assembling a group for creative thinking, try to come up with some unconventional things you could do throughout the session. Consider how you might kick off the session with something surprising, such as an overshare or providing instructions about the session in a novel way. Think about what unconventional behaviours or events you could plan to do throughout the session to continue to boost cohesion and creativity among the group.

Reframe procrastination

The next time you find yourself procrastinating, stop beating yourself up. Forgive yourself for procrastinating – that is, do the opposite of what you would normally do.

Reflect on your feelings towards the task you are avoiding. A large part of overcoming procrastination is learning how to manage a negative emotional state, such as feeling bored by a certain task.

Try to understand why you are experiencing negative emotions in relation to the task and consider how you could make it a more positive experience. Habitualising tasks that you find yourself avoiding can also help to take the emotion out of it.

REFLECTION
Look inside

When did you last get a check-up at the dentist or doctor? Hopefully, it was in the last year. Perhaps your visit was driven by a sore tooth. Or maybe you injured yourself exercising and needed someone to take a look.

It's usually obvious when something goes wrong with our body because it tells us so. It hurts or aches or itches. It alerts us to stop and get help.

If only the same were true about life. If our work or our relationship is progressively deteriorating, there is often not a specific incident that jolts us into action. We are like the apocryphal frog in boiling water. By the time we realise things are getting hot, we have potentially wasted several years of our life when an earlier pivot would have led to far greater fulfilment.

This section starts by looking at the importance of reflecting on the big picture. We will explore why you need to book yourself in for regular life check-ups, even when nothing is obviously aching or wrong.

We will then dive into the power of self-doubt, tackling feelings of inferiority, and conquering fears.

Eliciting feedback is, of course, critical in helping us reflect and improve ourselves, but unfortunately, most of us are not great at drawing out feedback that is useful. We are about to change all that with some practical ways to ask for and receive feedback that helps us grow.

We will learn a simple trick to help turn unhelpful self-talk into something more motivating, and we will finish on a high note – why we need to regularly remind ourselves that we will die.

Why you need to schedule regular life check-ups

Wharton Professor and organisational psychologist Adam Grant is routinely contacted by past students who have spent a couple of years out of university and are starting to question their career choices. They confess to Grant that they are miserable in their job and that they should have walked away a couple of years ago, but they didn't. And now they feel trapped. Instead of walking away from a role that was making them miserable, they felt that they had to stay because they had already sunk several years of their life into it.

Grant found himself suggesting to these students, 'Why don't you put a reminder in your calendar twice a year to do a life check-up?' In the same way people go to the doctor once a year for a check-up, even when it seems like nothing is wrong, he believes everyone should do the same with their career.

'Ask yourself: is this still the job that I want? Have I reached a learning plateau or a lifestyle plateau? Is this culture toxic?' he suggests. 'Don't do that every day, because then you're just going to be stuck in analysis paralysis and you'll never give the place you're in a chance. But if you do it a couple of times a year, maybe it'll save you from getting trapped in a place that you don't want to be.'

Grant takes his own advice and schedules regular life check-ups. 'I have a reminder in my calendar that pops up twice a year for a check-up. One is in July to do a rethinking of my teaching approach and what content I'm going to cover that semester. And the other pops up in January, when I think about what I want to be working on in terms of research and writing and podcasting.'

One of the projects Grant is best known for is hosting the *WorkLife* podcast for TED. The podcast was actually born from a life check-up. At the time, he felt like he was stagnating. He had just published his third book and was doing a lot of speaking and interviews and feeling like a human jukebox. 'I would give my performance and I would learn nothing because I was basically covering the same material as last time.'

He realised he needed to start learning again but he didn't want to commit to something as big as his next book. 'I just wanted to explore something that was a little smaller, interesting and important, but wasn't necessarily one big idea that deserved a whole book.'

And at around the same time, he had launched into some conversations with the TED team about ways that they might be able to collaborate on something that's more dialogue than monologue.

For Grant, podcasting was a great way to shake things up a little bit and explore smaller topics that were piquing his curiosity. *WorkLife* allows him to go to some of the most interesting workplaces on earth and talk to fascinating people. 'My goal is to learn, and then I can share what I've learned on the backend.'

Put it into action

1. Book a meeting with yourself twice a year and label it 'Life check-up'.
2. When the time comes, ask yourself:
   a. Am I in the right job? (If not, what is lacking? What do you want more of?)
   b. Have I reached a plateau? (If yes, what do you want to be learning over the next six–twelve months?)
   c. Am I energised by what I do? (If not, what sort of projects would you find energising?)

    d. Is the workplace culture one where I can thrive? (If not, what sort of a culture would be one where you could thrive and feel supported?)

3. Depending on your answers, write yourself a prescription (i.e., a plan) to address the areas for improvement.

4. Download a one-page life check-up one-page template to use for your next check-up at amantha.com/timewise

Use self-doubt as a strength, not a weakness

A little over twenty years ago, I received a phone call to tell me I had been accepted into the Doctorate of Organisational Psychology program at Monash University. My first thought upon receiving the call: there must have been an administrative error.

Turns out, there wasn't. I went on to become the youngest graduate from the program and register as an organisational psychologist. But it also turns out that I am not alone in experiencing Imposter Syndrome, which is the persistent thought that we are undeserving of our achievements. Scientific research has found that up to 82 per cent of us experience Imposter Syndrome. The other 18 per cent are probably too scared to admit it.

When I interviewed *Broad City* co-creator, co-writer and co-star Abbi Jacobson on *How I Work*, my stomach was doing somersaults. I had been a fan of Jacobson's work for years and had watched every single episode of her show. In my research for the interview, I had read that she suffered from a severe case of Imposter Syndrome during the earlier seasons of *Broad City*. I was curious to know if she still experienced it.

In short, her answer was 'yes'. She told me about experiences of speaking at an event or being on a panel and how she would feel cloaked in self-doubt.

'"What am I doing here? Why does anyone care what I have to say about this topic?" I get very nervous before performances or new things. Like I'm going to be exposed for not being good,' Jacobson told me.

But here's the thing: unlike most of us who interpret nerves and self-doubt as a bad thing, for Abbi, it's positive.

'I'm happy that I still get very nervous, even if I maybe shouldn't be. If there ever was a day where I was like, "Yeah, I should totally be here" – I don't want to be like that. I want to always be looking at myself and questioning where I am right now in my career. I want to be measuring how far I've come and know that there's still so much farther to go. Even if I am really confident in what I'm doing right now and the projects I'm working on, I still can be so much better.'

Stanford University Psychologist Alia Crum led research that found that when people perceive their self-doubts and nerves as being helpful, they feel inspired to learn and to grow when they experience these stressful thoughts. Because of this mindset that allows them to see stress as a positive, they believe that nerves actually improve their performance and productivity. In addition, people who adopt this mindset are more likely to learn from their mistakes and change in response to feedback.

Put it into action

1. Pause and reflect on your self-talk when it expresses itself as self-doubt.
2. The next time you experience self-doubt, try interpreting these feelings as a motivating force. Let them be a reminder that there is always room to grow.
3. Instead of shying away from the experience triggering the doubt, deliberately embrace it and remember that it's only through challenges that we can improve.

Stop trying to be the smartest person in the room

Cyan Ta'eed spent many years feeling like she wasn't as competent as many people perceived her to be. This was despite co-founding Envato, a Melbourne-based technology company worth over one billion dollars. You know – just a little side hustle.

'I spent a long time feeling like I was trying to cover up, feeling like I wasn't as intelligent and as capable as everyone maybe thought I was,' Ta'eed told me. At the age of twenty-seven, she had found herself running a fifty-person team at Envato. She felt deeply inexperienced and knew she had a lot to learn.

'We then went through a period where we had a lot of very experienced people coming into the business and I thought, "I'll step aside. The big kids are here now". And they said, "Don't worry, we've got this, we know how to do this."'

But slowly, Ta'eed realised that they didn't. She learned that there was something different about the way she did things that was valuable and useful and, in some cases, better. 'So I had to figure out what it was that was going on with me. I felt like I really needed to address it.'

Ta'eed, of course, had a classic case of Imposter Syndrome. To try to overcome it, she looked for role models – people who oozed an effortless confidence. And she didn't have to look far. 'Those two people were my best friend, Natalie Tam, and my husband. They were naturally confident and chilled out.'

One of the qualities they had in common was that they never

seemed to worry about asking questions that might make them look stupid. 'And I always worried about that,' she confessed.

'I needed to shift my thinking from wanting to seem like the smartest person in the room to wanting to leave the room *being* the smartest person. And it meant that I needed to ask questions constantly and I needed to not care whether it made me look like an idiot.'

On a more macro level, she realised that her Imposter Syndrome led to her shying away from opportunities that scared her. 'For a long time, I tried to avoid failing,' Ta'eed explained. 'But then I realised that I needed to start saying "yes" to opportunities even when they really scared me.'

Over time, Ta'eed forced herself to get comfortable failing and figuring out how to cope with that. She found that the more she did it, the less it became about her and the more it became about the concept that she was just trying to embark on new challenges.

'When you try to do really hard things that someone's never done before, oftentimes you fail. I've launched about ten start-ups and there's a lot you haven't heard about and don't know about because they didn't succeed and I closed them down.' So instead of fearing failure, Ta'eed approaches it head-on and embraces the potential obstacles ahead of her.

Put it into action

1. Reflect on your own self-censorship, such as when you might stop yourself from asking a question for fear of sounding stupid. Chances are, other people in the room want to ask the exact same question. Remember, you are doing everyone else a favour by asking your 'stupid' question.
2. As challenging as it can be, try to act in opposition to your fear. You might do this by reframing your self-talk, like Ta'eed did. Instead of trying to seem like the smartest person, Ta'eed planned to leave *being* a smarter person.

3. When reviewing opportunities to throw yourself into, consider whether you're scared by them. Are you hesitating to take it on because you are worried about failure? If the answer is 'yes', it's probably a good sign that you should lean into the challenge because it will be a great opportunity for growth.

Remember,
it's your story

A constant struggle I have with myself when interviewing guests on *How I Work* is deciding how much of myself to share in the interview. I oscillate between making it all about the guest versus sharing bits about my own working style where it relates to something a guest says.

The voice in my head says, 'People are tuning in for the guests, not for you, so shush' and as a result, I tend to keep my interviews primarily focused on my guests. But then, occasionally, I'll get advice to the contrary and re-think my whole approach.

One such advice-giver was renowned *New York Times* journalist Kara Swisher, who is also the host of one of my favourite podcasts, *Pivot*. She shared with me the best piece of career advice she had ever received. It was given to her when she was writing her first book about the story of AOL and how it became the world's biggest online company back in the 1990s.

'I was overwhelmed,' Swisher told me. 'I was a young reporter and I was good, but I was still very early in my career. And I was just beside myself. I interviewed all these people and there was so much information. There was just so much coming in and I didn't know quite how to organise it.'

Swisher called up a friend of hers who wrote true crime novels – the only person she knew who had written a book. Her friend was a fellow journalist who would cover a trial and then write a book about the story. 'I said, "I don't know what to do. I'm just going crazy".'

Her friend calmed her down and said, 'You're not writing the whole story of AOL. It's *your* story of AOL. What's your story? What do you want to say about it?'

After hearing those words of advice, it suddenly became easy. 'I was like, "Oh, it's not *the* story. It's *my* story. That's easy."' And to this day, when Swisher is struggling with something, she will remind herself: it's *her* story, not *a* story.

So now, especially when it comes to creative projects where there are often no rules and I don't know how much of myself to put into something, I return to Swisher's advice. And especially with *How I Work*, when I am struggling with how much of myself to share into an interview, I remind myself, 'It's not an interview with this guest, it's *my* interview with this guest'.

Put it into action

1. Think about a project you are working on where you are being guided by external standards or trying to conform to external norms. It might be a presentation for work, a creative project such as an article or blog post, or maybe even how you are planning to approach an important meeting.
2. Rather than trying to do things the 'right' way by following whatever 'rules' are in place, remember that the magic will come from doing it your way.

Transform fear into excitement with this simple question

Think back to a time when you tried to do something that scared you. Perhaps you had to give a high-stakes presentation in front of a big group of people. Maybe you worked up the courage to ask your boss for a pay rise. Perhaps you jumped out of a plane (hopefully with a parachute). Or maybe you were one of the participants in the spider experiment I described on page 166.

If you spoke to someone about how you were feeling in the lead-up to the event, chances are a well-meaning friend said to you, 'What's the worst that could happen?'

Michelle Poler has heard this advice hundreds of times. When she was doing her Masters in Branding back in 2015, she started a project to conquer one hundred fears in one hundred days. Her Masters project turned into a global movement that impacted millions of people and received coverage on the NBC's *Today* show, Fox News, CBS and CNN, to name a few.

When Poler was in the middle of her project, conquering fears such as performing stand-up comedy, cliff diving and swimming with sharks, people often tried to help her by asking 'What's the worst that could happen?'

While Poler could concede that perhaps she wouldn't die, there were many other worst-case scenarios this question would bring to mind. 'Maybe I won't die, but I will embarrass myself. I might fail. I might get rejected. I might hurt my ego and my self-esteem. There are many things that can go wrong whenever we take a risk.'

The key problem with the 'What's the worst that could happen?' question is that it serves to bring out the worst-case scenarios. So Poler realised that she needed to change the question.

'If we actually want to face a fear, and do it with the best attitude, we have to ask ourselves, "What's the best that can happen?" instead of "What's the worst?". When you think about the best that could happen, only the best-case scenarios will come to your mind. And this reminds you of the real reason why you thought that this was a good idea in the first place.'

When we think about the worst thing that could happen, our brain gets filled with negative thoughts and images. It only serves to ignite our worry or anxiety. However, when we imagine the best thing that could happen, it focuses us on the possibilities that could come from the scary thing we are about to do. We might get a pay rise, we might have a really positive impact on the crowd we are about to address, or we might feel a huge sense of pride (not to mention adrenaline) from having the courage to jump from a plane.

Research published in the *Journal of Positive Psychology* supports asking ourselves the question: What is the best thing that could happen? Duke University's Kathryn Adair Boulus, who led the research, found that when people thought about a positive event they hoped would happen in their future just six times in the space of a month, they reported feeling more resilient and less depressed compared to those who didn't focus on positive future events. Adair also found that for the 'positive future event' group, when they did experience disappointments, their feelings subsided more quickly. So the more confident we can feel about uncertainty, we not only feel happier in the present, but we are also more prepared for the setbacks that life inevitably throws at us in the future.

Put it into action

1. The next time you are feeling nervous or scared about an event or activity that you are about to do, ask yourself, 'What's the best that could happen?'.
2. Take a few minutes to write down your answers to really internalise the possibilities that having the courage to face a fear could have on your life.

The ideal time to seek feedback

You have just finished working on an important presentation that you have to deliver in two days' time to your leadership team. You've spent hours writing and polishing it. And finally, you're feeling like it's in a really good state. You send the presentation to a teammate to look over. You casually ask her to give any feedback she has for you. Unexpectedly, she sends you a shopping list's worth of criticism (she also clearly failed to read between the lines and realise that you were really just looking for compliments). In an instant, you go from feeling confident and proud of your work, to feeling miserable.

Feedback received at the wrong time can be extremely demotivating. Dan Heath, the bestselling author of books including *Made to Stick*, *The Power of Moments* and *Switch*, has experienced how demoralising ill-timed feedback can be.

'I think a lot of writers make the mistake of getting 90 per cent of the way there and then they start asking for feedback,' says Heath. 'And at that point, if you get negative feedback, you can't afford to take it on. Your instinct is going to be to push back and think, "Oh, well that's just nit-picking," or, "I can't afford to revisit that."'

Instead, Heath says the sweet spot for asking for feedback is roughly at the halfway or 60 per cent mark. 'Asking for feedback earlier in the process allows you the mental space to really rethink things if necessary.'

Scientists have investigated why this might be the case. They found that when people sought feedback on a speech or draft once it was

complete, their primary motivation for the input was to seek affirmation (after all, they're only human). In contrast, when people asked for feedback well before they had finished a project, their main motivation was to improve their work. So when we can adopt the mindset of striving to improve (as opposed to just wanting to demonstrate how great we are), research suggests we are more open to criticism and are thus more likely to embrace the feedback.

Put it into action

1. Avoid falling into the trap of asking for feedback too late in your process. Instead, when you reach the halfway mark, or a little over, think of that as the ideal time to seek feedback. This will allow you to reflect on your work more effectively without getting demotivated.

How to elicit feedback that's actually useful

While immersed in the day-to-day rhythm of writing this book, concurrently, I was trying to think of a title. Every so often, I would send a shortlist of potential titles to my editor for feedback. But to be honest, I wasn't really after feedback. I wanted my editor to say, 'That's the cleverest title I've ever heard! You are a book-naming legend!'

Scott Young, best-selling author of *Ultralearning*, believes that most people don't actually want feedback when they ask for it. They intuitively know feedback is good for them, but what they are really seeking is reassurance. But when it comes to using time wisely, sourcing valuable feedback is critical to producing the best possible outcome.

When Young was writing *Ultralearning*, he spoke to Avraham Kluger, who co-authored a meta-analysis on the impact of feedback on performance with Angelo DeNisi. Through a meta-analysis, Kluger found that when people ask for feedback, they don't really want it, and one-third of the time, feedback actually made their performance worse.

'The person says "I want feedback",' explains Young, 'But what they're really saying is, "I want you to say I did a great job". They're not really seeking to improve themselves.

'What Kluger found is that if you give people feedback when they don't actually want it, when they're not really seeking feedback, that it tends to backfire and not actually improve their performance. So the idea that you should give feedback to people is not necessarily helpful if that person doesn't want to actually use the information to improve.'

Young is often approached by budding writers who contact him asking for feedback. Young has adapted how he responds to these people, based on the research. 'When people ask me for feedback, usually my first question is, "What kind of feedback are you looking for?" And I'm hoping that when I ask that question to people, it will prompt them to reflect on more specific questions they can ask me rather than just asking for feedback in general.'

Young has found that this approach forces people to really reflect on what they are looking for, and it also enables him to be more helpful if he does take the time to provide feedback. What's more, he has also found that it puts him in a helping mindset, rather than a critical one, because the person will have identified something they think might need some work and they want him to point it out.

Dan Heath is also a big fan of asking for specific feedback. He never asks general questions such as 'What did you think of the book?' as he believes people might hold back to spare his feelings and thus not be 100 per cent honest. In addition, at the halfway mark, Heath doesn't want feedback about the core of the book. 'I don't know that you want to trust someone who's spent five hours thinking about your book over yourself who spent two years working on the book.'

But he says what you can trust is people's gut instinct about specific aspects of a project. He will ask questions such as 'What did you think about this specific part?' or 'Was this bit interesting?' or 'Which of these two things did you prefer?'

'I want to get feedback at a point in the cycle when I can use it. And I want to get feedback that's particular enough that I can really trust it.'

Put it into action

1. When asking for feedback, be specific about the type of feedback you want. For example, if it's a piece of writing, do you want someone to proofread it for typos, or to comment on whether it is engaging? If it's a presentation, do you want

people to give feedback on your content, your style, or whether you were funny?

2. When you are asked to provide feedback, ask the person what, specifically, they want feedback on. This will force the person to reflect on whether they genuinely want feedback, as opposed to reassurance. And it will also help you use your time more wisely when investing effort in providing feedback, since you'll be giving them what they truly want and will actually apply.

It's time to pay people to criticise you

We all know that feedback helps us grow. And receiving constructive or negative – not positive – feedback is what helps us grow the most. But here's the problem: many people shy away from giving negative feedback. We worry about hurting the other person's feelings, or perhaps we assume that the thing we want to provide feedback on is 'no big deal', so we forget about it and move on.

Perhaps you have participated in a training program on how to give feedback more effectively. I've been through several, none of which were helpful. And as a people-pleaser myself, the training did not make it easier for me to deliver feedback that I knew would be hard for the other person to hear. So what's the solution?

As one of the world's leading close-up magicians, performance feedback is critical to Simon Coronel. But Coronel is not your typical entertainer. He originally worked as an IT consultant for consulting firm Accenture, and studied psychology at university. As a result, he thinks a lot about human psychology when trying to refine his own performance.

One of the keys to a great magic trick is an audience's inability to work out how it was achieved. When Coronel tests a new illusion, he used to ask people if they could figure out the mechanics behind it. But audience members would err on the side of politeness and say they had no idea, even if they had a few.

To break through the politeness, Coronel started asking, 'If I offered you a million dollars to guess how this trick was done, what would you say?' He found that asking audience members this question invited them to reveal whatever was on their mind (even though they were dubious that Coronel had one million dollars to hand over to them). However, this question proved to be a useful one for a magician because if your audience can come up with something, it means that the trick is just that little bit less amazing, so Coronel could then work on improving it.

In his pursuit of feedback, and particularly of the critical variety, he took things a step further. 'I actually started getting out a little stack of dollar coins and setting them up on a table in the foyer of the theatre. I would say to people after the show, "I'll give you a dollar for every criticism you can make about the show. Every bad thing you can think of in any way and on any level." I was basically willing to pay for negative feedback. That's how much I actually wanted the constructive criticism.'

Coronel would ask people if there was anything that was weird about the show. Anything that was distracting. And if there was anything that was offensive, or that didn't make sense?

'I once received feedback that someone was distracted because my shoes weren't polished. And something like that matters just as much as the magic because everything in the show is part of the show. And it's the same in any business or with any product. Everything is part of the overall experience the person has when they engage with you or your business or your service.'

Put it into action

1. The next time you really want constructive feedback, consider paying people or offering them a gift. For example, you could offer to shout someone a coffee if they give you three bits of constructive feedback.

2. Where possible, ask for feedback as soon as they have engaged with what you are seeking feedback on. For example, if you want a critique of a presentation you delivered, ask for the feedback immediately afterwards. And, of course, extend the invitation for people to reach back out with any additional negative feedback if more comes to mind.

The power of
watching yourself back

If you live in Australia, you've probably seen Sandra Sully read the news. She has been doing it for thirty years. 'What a lot of people don't realise is that there is a real performance aspect to what you do,' explains Sully. 'I was told a long time ago that for every hour you're on television, it's the equivalent to about three hours' work because of the energy you use.'

Sully describes it as an intense hour with lots of peaks and troughs. She will receive news updates throughout the day and will even be writing updates during the time she is on air. And the adrenaline that accompanies reporting on a big story is enormous.

You would assume that more than three decades' worth of experience as a news presenter would make Sully believe there is little room for improvement. But on the contrary, Sully reviews her performance almost every night. She literally watches herself reading the news and looks for ways to improve.

'I appreciate the fact that you can always keep learning. I never think or know that I'm "there". I always believe I can be better. When you accept that there's a dramatic component to what you do, it's very easy to develop ticks without really realising it. It might be referencing a monitor, turning your head, developing an intonation, or pausing.'

Sully gives reading the introduction to a news story as an example. 'The first two paragraphs are structured around a number of phrases with keywords that make sense of the story. The introduction is written for a reason, and it has to be delivered with the right emphasis in the right space.'

Sully is also mindful that though she is in someone's home, they're not necessarily watching her. They might be in the kitchen preparing dinner and have the television on in the background. 'They're often just hearing me, so I need to emphasise the keywords that make sense of the story.

'My job is to make sure, at the end of the day, that I get it more right than wrong. I have to feel comfortable in myself that I'm consistently being the standard I'm proud of.'

In my role at Inventium, one of the most powerful things I have ever done is record presentations I have given and watch myself back. I remember the first time I did this, almost twenty years ago. It was part of a presentation skills training program I participated in, where we had to deliver a ten-minute presentation and watch the recording back. It was excruciating. Imagine fingernails scraping down a blackboard and multiply that discomfort by 10,000. But it was also a transformative use of time. I had so many distracting mannerisms and verbal ticks I was unaware of. And by making the unconscious conscious, I was able to eliminate the distractions so I could communicate with more impact.

In my role as a podcast host, my producer Kellie Riordan and I do 'air-checks', a term borrowed from radio. We regularly pick a ten- to fifteen-minute section of an interview and Kellie will tear it apart – in a good way – to take a really deep dive and analyse my technique and delivery, and identify what could be better. The air-check process has improved my skills as an interviewer and podcast host dramatically (at least, that's how it feels to me).

Put it into action

1. While you are probably not a newsreader, think about the key competencies that your job involves. Chances are that communication is part of it, whether it be written or oral.

2. Think about how you could 'watch yourself back' to improve your performance. If your job relies a lot on written communication, set aside time regularly to objectively review some of the key pieces you have written. If your job involves oral communication, consider recording yourself in meetings or giving presentations and, as horrific as it might be, watch the recording back and critique yourself. Look for verbal ticks or things that might be getting in the way of you communicating effectively.

A simple phrase to motivate yourself to do things you don't want to do

If you are a morning exerciser like me, you have probably started many days when you literally had to drag yourself out of bed, reluctantly put on your gym gear and force yourself out the door to go for a run. I exercise five mornings per week – it's become habitual. But I definitely have days when it's the last thing I want to do. My inner-sloth says, 'Just lie in bed a bit longer – it's so nice and warm in here! Please don't make me lift weights in the freezing cold garage on this horrible winter's morning! Please, no!'

But my inner sloth-tamer retorts, 'You have to exercise! Go! Now! C'mon, I said "go"!' And begrudgingly, I go and do it. Urgh.

But could there be a better way of talking to myself? A method that actually makes me want to go and exercise rather than feel as though I am being bossed around by a nasty little sloth-taming slavedriver? Turns out there is.

While competing in a 100-km ultramarathon in 2011, Turia Pitt was caught in a grassfire and suffered full thickness burns to 65 per cent of her body. But surviving is the least of her achievements. Turia has gone on to become a bestselling author, a two-time Ironman and a humanitarian. And in 2017, she gave birth to her first son, Hakavai.

After becoming a mum, she became aware of her own self-talk around feeling as if she 'had' to do certain things.

'I have to go clean his room or I have to prepare his food or have to wash his clothes,' Pitt would think to herself. 'When you tell yourself that you have to do things it's really easy for you to resent them and for them to feel like an obligation and something that you don't actually want to do.'

After reflecting on the impact that her inner voice was having, Pitt made a simple change. She started saying 'I get to'.

'"I get to pick up Hakavai, I get to play with Hakavai, I get to be around and I get to watch him as he grows up". And for me, just changing my language suddenly reminded me that it was an opportunity. It was a choice, and it was something that I got to be really grateful for.'

Pitt also started to use this strategy in her professional life. As part of her work, Pitt delivers a lot of keynote presentations. She often feels very nervous beforehand and gets stuck in her own head, undermining her own focus and confidence. She worries that she won't articulate herself clearly, or that people will think she is an idiot.

'I have to really stop and remind myself that it's not that I have to do a speech, but that I *get* to do a speech. It's a pretty awesome opportunity that a room full of people potentially want to listen to me and want to hear what I have to say.'

The effectiveness of the 'get to' strategy lies in the fact that it reframes the activity from being a chore to being a gift. It taps into intrinsic, instead of extrinsic, motivation. Usually, when we feel as though we have to do something, it's like an external force is telling us to do the activity: we don't have a choice. But when we *get to* do something, it reframes the activity into one over which we have control and choice: we are choosing to exercise, for example. And it makes our choice feel like it's in line with our own values and wishes.

Reframing the task reduces time wasted procrastinating, so it's a win-win: the task gets done and you feel happy about doing it.

Put it into action

1. Think about a behaviour that you know is good for you but that you have negative self-talk around. It might be a healthy habit you are trying to form, such as eating more vegetables

or sticking to an exercise regime. It might be about a work task you have been avoiding or procrastinating over. There is a good chance that you've been telling yourself that you have to do it.

2. Deliberately rephrase your self-talk into using the language 'I get to do this task'. And consider how doing the task aligns with what matters to you, such as being healthy or doing a great job at work.

Remind yourself that you will die

As the co-founder of global fintech, Finder.com, Fred Schebesta deliberately makes his calendar visible to his global workforce of several hundred people. But if any of his employees looked closely, they would notice something unusual written in it.

Once a month, a reminder pops up in Schebesta's calendar that says Memento Mori, an old Latin phrasing meaning 'remember you must die'.

'I remind myself every month that one day I will die,' explains Schebesta. No, he is not a sadomasochist. Instead, the reminder leads to him checking in with himself and asking questions such as whether he is spending his time in a way that aligns with his values and what matters to him. If the answer is 'no', it prompts him to make a change.

Cyan Ta'eed, co-founder of billion-dollar technology company Envato, used to have a similar routine. 'I had an app on my phone for a while which told me I was going to die, and it told me this five times a day. It would basically come up with notifications that remind me that I will die.'

For Ta'eed, the reminder served to help her be present and make every moment count. It also helped her stop worrying about things that just didn't matter.

Roman philosopher Seneca, one of the adherents to the Stoic movement, wrote about this in one of his essays, 'The Shortness of Life':

It is not that we have a short time to live, but that we waste a lot of it. Life is long enough, and a sufficiently generous amount has been given to us for the highest achievements if it were all well invested. But when it is wasted in heedless luxury and spent on no good activity, we are forced at last by death's final constraint to realise that it has passed away before we knew it was passing. So it is: we are not given a short life but we make it short, and we are not ill-supplied but wasteful of it [. . .] Life is long if you know how to use it.

At the time of writing, there are several apps you can download onto your phone for frequent death reminders. WeCroak will send you a reminder several times a day at unpredictable moments. And Countdown App will give you a countdown of how much longer you have left on earth, based on your age, gender, BMI, smoking habits and where you live.

Put it into action

1. Schedule a regular reminder of your mortality. You might even book a meeting with yourself to deliberately take time out to reflect on the choices you are making in your life, both on a micro, day-to-day level, as well as on a macro level.
2. During this time, reflect on how present you are being in your life and whether you are making the most of your time on this planet.

REFLECTION
A summary

Schedule life check-ups
Book a twice-yearly life check-up with yourself. When the time comes, ask yourself: Am I in the right job? Have I reached a plateau? Am I energised by what I do? Is the workplace culture one where I can thrive?

Depending on your answers, put in place a plan to address the areas for improvement.

Use your self-doubt as a strength
The next time you experience self-doubt, try interpreting those feelings as a motivating force – let them be a reminder that there is always room to grow. Instead of shying away from the experience triggering the doubt, deliberately embrace it and remember that it's only through challenges that we can improve.

Reframe your self-talk
Become aware of your own self-censorship when around other people. Act in opposition to your fear by reframing your self-talk. For example, instead of trying to *seem* like the smartest person, attempt to leave *being* a smarter person.

When reviewing opportunities to throw yourself into, ask yourself if you're scared by them. If the answer is 'yes', take them on because they will present the circumstances for growth.

Do it your way

Think about a project you are working on where you are being guided by external standards or trying to conform to external norms. Rather than trying to do things the 'right' way by following whatever rules are in place, remember that the magic will come from doing it your way.

What's the best that could happen?

The next time you are feeling nervous or scared about something, ask yourself, 'What's the best that could happen?'. Take a few minutes to write down your answers to really internalise the possibilities that having the courage to face a fear could have on your life.

Ask for feedback at 60 per cent

Avoid falling into the trap of asking for feedback too late in the process. Instead, when you are about halfway through a task, or a little over, seek out feedback.

Be more specific about the type of feedback you ask for (and give)

When asking for feedback, be specific about the type of feedback you want. For example, if it's a piece of writing, do you want someone to proofread it for typos, or to comment on whether it is engaging?

When you are asked to provide feedback, ask the person what they want feedback on. This will force the person to reflect on whether they genuinely want feedback, versus reassurance.

Pay for criticism

The next time you really want constructive feedback, consider paying people or offering them a gift in exchange for a critique. And wherever possible, ask for feedback as soon as they have engaged with what you are seeking feedback on.

Watch yourself back

Think about how you could 'watch yourself back' to improve your performance. If your job relies a lot on written communication, set aside time regularly to review some of the key pieces you have written. If your job involves oral communication, consider recording yourself in meetings or presentations and watch the recording back to critique yourself.

I 'get' to

Think about a behaviour that you know is good for you but that you have negative self-talk around. It might be a healthy habit you are trying to form, such as having more alcohol-free nights or cutting back on sugar. It's likely that you are telling yourself that you have to do it.

Deliberately rephrase your self-talk using the language 'I get to do this task'. And consider how doing the task aligns with what matters to you, such as making healthy choices or doing a great job at work.

The Death Reminder

Schedule a regular reminder of your mortality. During this time, reflect on how present you are being in your life and whether you are making the most of your time.

CONNECTION
Build better relationships

In the world according to COVID, connecting with others has never been more important – and in many cases, more challenging. Given that many of us don't work in the same physical space as our teammates every day, it's easy to feel both physically and emotionally distant.

But to be happy at work and successful in your career, human connection is critical. Time well spent in the presence of others not only makes for better collaborations at work, but is also a guaranteed way to bring more joy to your life.

This section kicks off with a simple way to fast-track people getting to know you. We will then have a look at how to use clothing (and in this case, a T-shirt) to achieve cut-through with your communication, as well as the power of giving an unexpected gift.

I often feel as if I work as an island, but we'll take a look at why that's just not true and how to embrace the power of collaboration.

We will then dive into networking, everyone's favourite work activity! We will look at how to build solid relationships swiftly and the tricks and techniques to make networking easier and enjoyable (yes, really), even if you think spending the day picking small bits of fluff out of your clothes dryer's filter would be more fun than a few minutes of talking to strangers and engaging in small talk.

This section finishes with why humour is so important and how you can use it to your advantage when building relationships with others.

Why you need a one-page operating manual

Have you recently purchased a new gadget or appliance? Perhaps you've started using an updated piece of software? I'm imagining it came with an operating manual (not that you read it, of course. You've got better things to do). And when something goes wrong with said product, as it probably will sometime in the future, you'll definitely be searching for the operating manual then (and probably not being able to find it anywhere, damn it!).

But what about humans? We are far more complex than machines, but unfortunately, we have no operating manual to speak of. Unless, of course, you have met Darren Murph.

Murph is Head of Remote for global software company GitLab. And he has created his own operating manual, accessible by anyone with an internet browser. No, Murph is not part-human, part-machine. He is a very amicable and charismatic human. He calls it his README page, a play on a term that is used to describe a form of computer software documentation (and who doesn't appreciate a good computer programming joke?).

'My README page is an operating manual of how you can quickly get up to speed about working with me,' Murph describes. 'It explains how I like to be communicated with, what I hope to learn in working with you, and what you need to know about me. Things like personality type, my working style and when I generally prefer to work.'

He explains that the biggest benefit of having this page is to scale knowledge. 'If you're working with me for the first time and we've never met in person, we might not even know what each other looks like. It's probably going to take quite a few hours at best to build some sort of rapport. And there will be a lot of answering questions back and forth for us to get an understanding of each other.'

Reading Murph's README page in advance of working with him only takes a couple of minutes, but you'll learn more in those few minutes than it would normally take in the two weeks, or longer, to understand a co-worker you know nothing about. Creating an operating manual about yourself allows people you work with to know exactly how to get the best out of you and what your work preferences are. They will also have a better understanding of how you're reacting to them once you've started collaborating.

Murph got the idea from the CEO of GitLab, Sid Sijbrandij. Sijbrandij has his own online operating page where he lists his major flaws, his strengths, feedback he has received from his direct reports, and competencies he's actively working to improve upon.

There are several key areas that Murph recommends everyone cover in their operating manual. First, describe your strengths and weaknesses and some of the qualities that make you, you. Describing your working style is also important. This might include your values and personality traits, as well as your peeve points.

Including how you like to be communicated with is also critical. For example, Murph prefers asynchronous communication. 'I really

like written communication. If you can engage with me over text, instead of jumping straight into a voice or video call, I generally prefer that. But that is not the case for everyone. And this is why it is very useful to have that written down so that there are as few misinterpretations as possible.'

Put it into action

1. To create your one-page operating manual, answer the following questions to get started:
   - What are your strengths? How can someone bring these out in you?
   - What are your weaknesses? What tends to bring these out?
   - How should people best communicate with you?
   - What are your pet peeves?
   - What do people misunderstand about you?
2. You might want to then add more details about yourself or take inspiration from Murph's README page, but these questions and your answers will provide a solid foundation.
3. To help make your operating manual even richer (and more accurate), ask five–ten people who have worked with you closely:
   - What brings out the best in me?
   - What brings out the worst in me?
   - What are my blind spots?
   - What do you wish you had known about me when we first started working together?

   Feed these responses into fleshing out your operating manual further.
4. Decide how you want to share your operating manual. You could create a Word document and share it with your team and anyone new you start working with. Or, like Murph, you could put it online for the world to see (see page 304).
5. Download a template for creating your one-page operating manual at amantha.com/timewise

Use an item of clothing to transform behaviour

Finding a communication channel that can cut through the clutter can be challenging. We are bombarded with emails, phone calls and meetings every day. But ex-President of Pinterest Tim Kendall discovered it within his wardrobe.

Prior to working at Pinterest, Kendall was the Director of Monetisation at Facebook. 'I remember when I was at Facebook, it was 2009, which was a seminal year for the business,' Kendall recalled. 'Mark Zuckerberg showed up to work on January 4th or 5th, and he was wearing a tie. As you can imagine, for Mark Zuckerberg that stands out. He said, "I'm wearing this every day for the rest of the year because this is a serious year".'

This gesture made a big impression on Kendall. 'All he was doing was wearing a tie every day, but the impact and the symbolism of that to the folks who were working with him and for him and around him was huge.'

Zuckerberg's act of wearing a tie had such a significant impact on Kendall that when he moved to Pinterest and became its president in 2015, he thought about how he could use his own wardrobe to deliver a message.

At the time of becoming president, Pinterest had around 15 million users. The organisation had set a target of hitting 200 million users within the space of a few years (you know, just a handful more). To achieve this, the company would have to focus.

Kendall recalls an anecdote about Jony Ive, the designer who brought us the iMac, the iPod and the iPhone at Apple, about the importance of focus. Ive was renowned for saying that focus is having three things that in every part of your body you just feel like you have to do, but only picking one.

'I wanted everyone to remember that most people, and I'm guilty of this myself, delude themselves into thinking that they're focused. They tell themselves, "I have a list of twenty things that I could do, twenty projects that I could do, twenty product features that I could build". And they cut the list in half and say, "I'm so focused". But real focus is taking those twenty things and only doing one.'

To communicate this message to his growing company, Kendall stood up at an all-staff meeting with a T-shirt that had the word 'focus' written across it. 'I got in front of the company and said, "I'm going to wear this T-shirt until we have 200 million users".'

Interestingly, research has found that symbols such as words and pictures can indeed transform behaviour. In one unusual study led by Professor Amanda Shantz from the University of St Gallen, employees at a fundraising call centre were given an information pack about their jobs. Half of the packs had a photo of a female athlete running triumphantly, while the other packs did not. Staff who received the information pack with the female runner raised a larger amount of funds across the day, compared to the group who had not received the

photo. Somehow, the running woman picture unconsciously transformed their behaviour.

Kendall ended up wearing the T-shirt until he left the company in January 2018, around four years later. (From a personal hygiene perspective, it's worth noting that Kendall printed a large number of these T-shirts.)

'I think when you are a leader at a company – and as the company grows from tens of people to hundreds of people and then thousands of people – what you have at your disposal to communicate to people, and illustrate symbolically where your head is, the universe of that stuff just shrinks, especially as the company grows.'

Put it into action

1. If you have an important message to communicate to your staff, try to avoid defaulting to the usual suspects such as emails and all-staff meetings. Yawn.
2. Instead, think about something outside the usual communication channels that will cut through the noise and connect with your audience. It may be your wardrobe, or with the move to more virtual meetings, perhaps even your video background or a prop that you have in all video calls.

The power of the unsolicited gift

A couple of years ago, auctioneer and co-founder of Gary Peer real estate agency, Phillip Kingston, was auctioning a property in inner-city Melbourne on the seventh floor of an apartment block. He remembers it being a charming building that held around fifty apartments. He was waiting in the lift lobby when, just above the 'up' button, he noticed a sign that was laminated and sitting directly above the button so you could not miss it.

'There was a smiley face on this sign, with a paragraph about how a smile can change the world and, as a community in this building, let's always remember to smile at other people who we see in the lift,' recalls Kingston. 'So many people, when they're dealing with others at work, forget to smile. Nothing appals me more than going into a cafe and looking at a line of people waiting for a coffee when no one talks to each other. They're all just looking at their phone.'

Kingston says that humour and getting people to smile on auction day can make a huge difference to the selling process. When people laugh, there is a physiological change and people feel better and more open. 'A smile or a laugh can completely change the dynamics of a situation.'

Having attended many of Kingston's auctions in Melbourne for myself, I can say that they feel more like a stand-up comedy show than your regular dull, monotonous auction. Several years ago, I took my daughter Frankie, who was four years old at the time, to see Kingston in action (yes, that's the kind of zany action-packed life

I lead – attending auctions just for fun on weekends). He saw us in the crowd, and mid-auction, he walked over to his car, pulled out a gift-wrapped present, and came over to us. He handed the present to my daughter. Frankie immediately unwrapped it and discovered a box of chocolates inside. It goes without saying that Kingston immediately became Frankie's hero, and she returned the favour with an enormous toothy grin while the crowd chuckled.

On auction day, Kingston thinks a lot about how he can bring in humour and happiness to get a better result for his clients.

'I love the unsolicited gift,' Kingston told me. 'I love the surprise that when I go to my car and I bring out something that's beautifully wrapped and the buyer or the person doesn't know what it is, it just changes us chemically.'

My team at Inventium have used this strategy several times in recent years. One of the ways we have applied it is when we lost big pitches. Rather than go off and mope, we do the unexpected. We send the people who rejected us a little gift and a note saying we hope we get to work with them in the future.

Another tradition we started at Inventium is Happy January. Instead of doing the predictable thing of giving clients a Christmas gift, we send them a card and gift in January. In full transparency, the ritual actually started back in the early days of Inventium when I ran out of time to send Christmas gifts to clients (you know, actually prior to Christmas). So I sent them in January instead.

Every year since then, for over a decade, we surprise our clients in January when not much else is going on gift-wise. Occasionally, this act has led to clients reaching out to us to quote on new work or has been a trigger for them referring other people our way. While this has been a pleasant surprise for *us*, it has shown me firsthand that a little bit of thoughtfulness and time spent in maintaining relationships is an investment in possible future rewards.

Put it into action

1. Look for opportunities to surprise people with an unsolicited gift. Instead of giving gifts at predictable times, give them when people least expect it.

Stop thinking of yourself as an island

Even though I have a team of ten people at Inventium, I often feel as if I work as an island. Most of my work tasks feel like solo missions: writing, researching, speaking, podcasting. And while I have people around me who help with every one of those endeavours – and indeed, I couldn't do what I do without them – it rarely occurs to me to proactively look for help when I am struggling with something. Which is why Marcus Buckingham's weekly ritual stuck with me.

Marcus Buckingham is a global expert on employee engagement. He has written several bestselling books on the topic and runs a consultancy that helps companies around the globe. Like me, Buckingham's work involves a lot of writing, researching and speaking – but he deeply understands the power of teams.

When I spoke to him, he had just finished a big piece of research across nineteen countries and many different industries. 'If you were to ask what is the most defining characteristic of work, it would be that we work in teams,' Buckingham told me. 'Nobody works alone. Even if your financial arrangements are that you're an individual contractor, we are all connected and so work is always teamwork. Eighty-three per cent of people say that they do most of their work in teams.'

While you may have individual flashes of genius over the course of a week, Buckingham says that almost everything that you're going to try to do this week at work will involve leaning into, relying on and calling upon the strengths of somebody else. 'And, of course, you can do so much more together than you can do alone.'

Buckingham used this insight to shape a weekly routine he now applies religiously. At the start of every week, he spends about fifteen minutes reflecting on what his priorities are for the week, and based on the answer to that question, he asks himself, 'Whose help do I need?'

I remember being surprised when I heard this question. It's not something I think I have ever asked myself.

'It's such a simple rhythm. The world moves really quickly, but if I can do that every week, it becomes a way to be super intentional about what's important this week.

'Thinking every single week about whose help you need is not only elevating in terms of thinking about other people and how you can involve them, but it's also just pragmatic. You're going to have to work with others. So you might as well think intentionally about who those others are.'

Anticipating from whom you might need help, and proactively asking for it, is a far smarter use of time than making last-minute, reactive requests.

Put it into action

1. At the beginning of each week, get clear on your priorities or goals for the week ahead.
2. Avoid thinking of yourself as an island, or feeling like you must do everything yourself. Instead, ask yourself "Whose help do I need?" These people might be in your immediate team or outside of it – it doesn't matter. What matters is that you acknowledge to yourself that you can find help to achieve your goals, and that no one is expecting you to get it done on your own.

Why you need to become an extreme giver

I imagine Emma Isaacs' digital rolodex reading like a who's who of thought leaders. As the founder and Global CEO of Business Chicks, an organisation that supports tens of thousands of businesswomen globally, she has attracted some of the biggest names in the world to speak to its members. Richard Branson, Seth Godin, Nicole Kidman, Julia Gillard, Brené Brown and Sir Bob Geldof have all graced her stages.

It would be easy to see these people as in your life for the event only, but Isaacs is a consummate relationship-builder.

'I always see relationships as a long-term play. It's not as if I secure them, and then I chew them up and spit them out,' says Isaacs. And while it's easy to think this long-term play simply means putting them on your e-newsletter list or connecting with them on LinkedIn, for Isaacs, it's something completely different.

'It's about being there at meaningful times in their life.' For example, Isaacs will make a note of their birthday or when they are releasing their next book. She has even been known to send authors a cake with their new book cover printed on it in icing, accompanied by a personal, hand-written note. A clever and delicious strategy for building relationships.

Isaacs also reflects on how she can genuinely support people. She leaves endorsements on LinkedIn as well as book reviews on Amazon. 'I can guarantee you every single author out there is looking at the Amazon reviews and they know exactly who has gone on and commented and rated them.'

Isaacs will also make a point of reaching out every now and again and asking simple questions such as: What do you need right now? Is there anything I can do for you? How can I support you?

One of the people she has formed a strong bond with over the years is Richard Branson. The relationship started when he spoke at a Business Chicks event, but it blossomed into the pair working together in various iterations for more than a decade. 'I've supported his philanthropic work. I've gone to South Africa and I've been a mentor at the Branson School of Entrepreneurship. I've done work with his centres in the British Virgin Islands. And so I'm always asking how can I be a meaningful support to these people and give them value.'

Isaac's default is to think about how she can give. She believes that people can smell it a mile off (and it's not a floral Chanel No. 5 type smell) when you just want something from someone for your own benefit with no consideration of their needs.

'I'm always thinking, "How can I connect people? How can I give value? How can I join the dots with what people need?" It's this constant monologue that goes on in my head of how can I be of service to people.' Your future self will thank you for investing time in proactive acts of kindness in the present.

Put it into action

1. When trying to build a long-term relationship with someone, adopt a mindset of generous and highly personalised giving.
2. Keep an eye out for key milestones in that person's life, such as starting a new job, having a child or achieving something significant at work, to name a few.
3. Think about how you can support them or give them something meaningful beyond a generic email or 'like' on social media. And remember, personalised cakes always go down a treat.

How to be a better networker – without meeting new people

'I love networking and making small talk with strangers,' said no one ever. Luckily, Marissa King, a Professor of Organisational Behaviour at the Yale School of Management, who literally wrote the book on the topic – *Social Chemistry* – has a weekly ritual to make networking a little more enjoyable.

King explains that there is extraordinary power in our existing networks. And arguably, the most impactful thing that most people can do to improve their network is to reinvigorate dormant ties. Dormant ties are people who you might not have seen in two or three years, or even longer.

Research led by Daniel Levin from Rutgers Business School examined the benefits of reaching out to dormant ties. The researchers asked people to make a list of ten current connections and ten people they haven't reached out to in two or three years. Participants were then asked to get back in touch with these people for advice or help with a project. Levin and his colleagues found that dormant ties were extraordinarily powerful in that they not only provided more creative ideas to people but also the trust had endured within those relationships.

King applied this research to design a ritual that she now carries out every Friday. 'I write down the names of two or three people. And I reach out to them just to say, "Hey, I'm thinking about you". Sometimes, I will have an ask or something I'm hoping to get out of it, like feedback or a question. But most of the time it's just, "Hey, I'm thinking about you". And that, for me, has been a source of great joy but it's also been extraordinarily helpful.'

Before starting this ritual, King was hesitant. 'I thought "Oh my God, isn't this going to be awkward?"' And personally, I'd be having the exact same thought, too. But it turns out, it wasn't.

'The more you do it, the more you realise that this is actually great. It's also helpful for me to imagine myself being in the other person's shoes. So if I imagine I received this email, would I be happy to receive it? And the answer is almost always "yes".'

King thinks about how she can be helpful to the people she is re-establishing contact with. And for her, there are three ways she can achieve this.

The first is to say "thank you". 'We know that gratitude is extremely powerful as a source of connection. So I think, "Is there a mentor who comes to mind right now or someone who gave me a piece of advice a couple of years ago or served as a role model?" And I simply reach out to them and thank them for what they've done.'

While this might seem inconsequential, research has found that people tend to underestimate the effects of saying 'thank you' and giving someone a compliment. In one study, people either gave or received praise from someone else. They were then asked to estimate how positive they would feel after giving or receiving these kind words. The researchers found that people significantly underestimated the degree to which their compliment would boost the mood of the other person. (And can I just say, dear reader, how radiant you are looking today?)

King's second reason for reaching out to people in her existing network is to share something she thinks the other person might enjoy, such as a podcast or an article. 'There are lots of things that we all have to give and just saying, "I'm thinking of you" is in many ways a gift, too.'

The final reason is to ask for help, which she also believes can be a gift. People enjoy feeling that their expertise matters and research shows that when we are asked to help someone else, it makes us feel closer to the person to whom we're offering assistance.

King says that despite the fact she is reaching out to people with whom she has had no contact for several years, she almost always receives a reply. 'I can't even think of a time when I haven't,' she admits.

The impact of her networking ritual has been huge, especially during 2020 when she spent most of the year in lockdown due to COVID.

'Particularly during the past year, it's been a lifesaver. It has allowed me to feel connected during moments when I didn't feel as connected as I possibly could be.' King's husband also adopted the ritual and found a new job, even though he wasn't looking for one. It was his dream job working with an amazing group of people, which was a game-changer for their family.

Time spent nurturing relationships with existing connections can not only lead to rewarding exchanges, but also to potentially trans-formative opportunities.

Put it into action

1. Set aside time once a month (or you could emulate King by making this a weekly activity) to write down two or three people with whom you haven't had contact for a few years.
2. Think about how you could be helpful to them. You might want to say thank you for something they did, share something with them that they might like or even ask them for advice on something you are currently working on.

A trick to building rapport fast

Building a connection with people quickly can have so many benefits for our careers. It can help us create improved working relationships with our colleagues, it can help close a sale, and it can help extend our networks. Some people make rapport-building seem effortless – it's as if they have charisma oozing out of every pore. The good news is, making a connection and breaking down barriers is a skill that can be learned.

David 'Kochie' Koch has been the co-host of top-rating breakfast television show *Sunrise* for nearly two decades. Part of his job involves interviewing celebrities, frequently very high-profile ones. But the challenge with interviewing famous people is that they have had media training, they have go-to talking points, and they often put up a facade when talking to the media.

For Kochie, finding strategies to build a strong connection in a short space of time is key to conducting a great interview. And from his years of interviewing, he's found a strategy that rarely fails.

'I always ask them about their upbringing [when he interviews them on-air]. Their relationship with brothers and sisters, their mum and dad, what they did together as a family. And that helps me to get a better handle on them,' he explains.

'It doesn't matter whether you're eighteen or eighty. You are a product of your family upbringing and you never, ever lose it. You can think you can, and you can pretend that you're a different person, but you never are. And that's where I always go to.'

Asking about family is a great human leveller. We all have one (in some way, shape or form), and we all have interesting stories to share. Yet it's rarely a go-to topic of conversation when you first meet someone, and it's definitely not a place that celebrities expect bite-sized television interviews to go.

'Very few people expect to ask you about their family. For example, we had Charli XCX on *Sunrise* the other day. Her new album cover is a bit racy. It's a nude photo of her. She was talking about that and I asked, "What does your mum think of it?" And she said, "I had to ring her up beforehand. I was a bit embarrassed and nervous to call her." And that showed the human side of her and the frailty of her.'

Kochie continued to go down the family route with Charli XCX. In his research, he found that her parents lent her money to record her first album. He asked her whether she had paid them back. 'She said, "Oh, no I haven't". And I joked, "Well that's not being a very good daughter, is it?" It brought down that wall of media training and made her like anybody else. Like, who hasn't borrowed money from their parents?'

Put it into action

1. When you are next trying to build a connection with someone in a professional setting, resist the urge to go straight to work-related topics. Instead, ask them about their family or their upbringing. By talking about childhood and family – experiences we've all had – you'll be able to build stronger and more human connections faster.

How to avoid small talk when meeting new people

From the outside, you would think Kevin Rose is supremely confident. He was an angel investor in Facebook, Twitter and Square, and founded the social news site Digg. He hosts one of the top-ranking podcasts in America, *The Kevin Rose Show*, and is also a partner at venture capital firm True Ventures. Not exactly an underachiever. Yet Rose describes himself as socially awkward, and indeed, being in places where he doesn't know people can fill him with nerves.

In addition to social awkwardness, Rose hates small talk. So he thought about strategies to help make it easier to talk to new people (as well as ones he knows) and avoid boring small talk.

'I try to find something that is not small talk but is a mutual kind of interest. And there's a bunch of wacky things that I'm into and so when people say, "What have you been up to lately?" or "What's new?" I respond with something like how I am trying to inoculate tree trunks to help grow lion's mane mushrooms. And typically, someone responds with, "Wow, tell me more" or they will share one of their wacky interests with me. It's something that is fun to talk about versus just being like, "Oh, the weather sucks".'

Before attending events, Rose will spend time consciously thinking about the interesting things he has been doing, and what might be of interest to who he will potentially be meeting.

He also reflects on the types of people he wants to connect with, which are typically people who are always exploring new things and are lifelong learners, like him. He deliberately thinks about questions that will bring these things out in someone, such as 'What are you into these days?' and 'What are you trying that's new and exciting?'

Research from Washington University backs up the efficacy of Rose's strategy. Associate Professor Cheri Levinson and her colleagues found that when people think about their unique experiences, stories and qualities, they reported feeling less anxious during social gatherings. Becoming more aware of our distinctive characteristics makes us less vulnerable to social anxiety.

Finally, Rose has found that people usually have a book to recommend, which can be another great way to avoid small talk. 'I always like to say to people that I'm looking for a new book to read. So I ask them, "What's a book that you've read in the last six months that you're really excited about or you could share with me?" People typically have something they're pretty stoked on.'

Adopting this technique when meeting people for the first time allows the conversation to go in unexpected directions. And even if you don't spend much time together, avoiding small talk can lead to useful and rewarding exchanges – a much wiser use of everyone's time.

Put it into action

1. The next time you have a social engagement coming up where you don't know anyone particularly well, think about three to five things you are doing that are novel or unique.
2. When someone asks you, as they inevitably will, "What have you been up to?", respond with one of these things. An interesting conversation will no doubt flow from there.
3. If you are like Rose and value connecting with people who are also lifelong learners (or mushroom growers), ask people, "What are you trying that's new and exciting". You could also ask, "What's a podcast or audiobook that you've listened to in the last six months that you're really excited about?"

Make meeting new people at events less terrifying

I attended my second TED conference back in 2019. If you have never been to 'TED proper' as it is sometimes referred to (well, at least by me), imagine a group of 2000 of the world's highest achieving people gathered in a huge convention centre. And they all seem to be besties but you don't know a soul (other than through seeing them on the television or reading their books or hero-worshipping them from afar). Intimidating, much?

Jerry Dischler is the Vice President of Product Management at Google, where he leads the Ads team. TED2019 was his first TED conference. Being on the introverted end of the spectrum, he was looking for strategies to make meeting 2000 strangers less intimidating. He also wanted to get the most out of being surrounded by all these fascinating, over-achieving strangers.

Dischler ended up meeting someone at the conference who gave him a great strategy. 'This person was a self-declared introvert who did not seem introverted at all. I asked him "How do you do this?" And so he says, "I approach it like a video game, actually." So he pretends to be an extroverted character in a video game and he scores points by talking to new people.'

Turning something from being scary into being fun is an effective way to change behaviour. Humans are motivated by feeling a sense of progress, and scoring points for meeting strangers is a clear way of making progress. In addition, the opportunity to score points distracts us from the fear, and at worst, paralysis, that can come with the idea of having to introduce yourself to people who you have never spoken to before in your life.

Playing a game like this is essentially a way of tricking ourselves to act more outgoing and socially confident. Interestingly, if more introverted people act in an extroverted manner and undertake activities associated with extroversion such as going to a new exercise class, a community event or volunteering at a place where they don't know anyone, their mood has been shown to improve.

In one study, a group of people were asked to participate in conversations with others. Immediately before the discussions, some participants were told to act as if they were extroverted; they were instructed to act bold, assertive, spontaneous and talkative. Other students were told to act as if they were introverted and appear quiet, timid and reserved. The students who acted like an extrovert experienced more positive emotions. And they also seemed more excited, interested and positive to onlookers.

As a proud introvert myself, I feel compelled to point out that being an introvert is still awesome in many ways (so, fellow introverts: don't go trying to change yourself) – but in certain situations, these tactics can be beneficial when spending time with people you don't know well. You will not only feel happier but will also form stronger bonds with those you speak to.

Put it into action

1. The next time you are at an event and feeling nervous, turn the experience into a game.
2. Think about a reward system that you will find motivating. This could be as simple as scoring points in an imaginary game, or it might be a tangible reward such as taking yourself out for a nice meal or a massage if you speak to a particular number of new people.
3. Set yourself a goal. In the case of a networking event, you might have the goal of scoring five points, where you get

one point per stranger you meet and who gives you their contact details.

4. Reward yourself once you hit the goal. Associating the reward with the behaviour that you found scary will help to reduce the fear you experience and increase the enjoyment you feel from that behaviour, in this case from networking.

A simple numbers trick to make networking easier

I avoid business events and conferences like the plague. (In fact, the only time you'll see me at an event is if I happen to be speaking at it). I hate that feeling of walking into a large conference hall and seeing a sea of strangers. Everyone seems to be having an amazing time and connecting with long-lost friends, whereas I feel like a social pariah. And I am always at a loss as to how I will infiltrate the crowd and find even one person who might want to talk to me.

Marissa King hates networking, yet somewhat ironically, has dedicated more than fifteen years to researching social networks. King is a Professor of Organisational Behaviour at the Yale School of Management and wrote the book *Social Chemistry*, which explores the science behind our networks.

Like me (and possibly everyone else on the planet), King really dislikes entering a room full of strangers and having to strike up a conversation with someone she doesn't know. But luckily, some of her research can help us out. 'What we know from research is that people don't form walls or oceans. They actually tend to clump together in small groups,' explains King.

'So really, it's not an ocean of people, it's only little islands. Then the question is "Now that I know they're islands and things feel a bit more manageable, what am I going to do next?" What researchers have found is that people almost always interact in groups of two, or dyads. It's really the most fundamental unit of human interaction. We have two eyes and we have two ears and our hearing does

something that's known as the cocktail party effect – it homes in on a single voice.'

For King, this means that when she looks at the islands of people, she is looking for a group that has an odd number. 'It might be three, five, seven. It doesn't really matter. If there's an odd number of people, then there's someone who really isn't a part of the conversation and they are likely looking for a conversational partner. And so that's a very basic strategy that has become critical for me to start to navigate a lot of the social anxiety I feel in these types of situations because it gives me direction.'

Gone will be the days of standing around wasting time waiting for an 'in'. You'll now be able to easily connect with new people, while simultaneously helping that third wheel who might be feeling left out.

Put it into action

1. The next time you are at an event where you don't know anyone or you want to meet new people, look for groups of three people (or any odd number will do).
2. Approach these groups and identify the person who is on the outer (one of them will be). Try to break off into a one-on-one conversation with this person.

Why you need to send funnier emails – and how to do it

What percentage of the emails you receive are a bit dull? Do they contain predictable phrases such as 'Following up on our discussion, here are my thoughts', 'Please circle back to me once you have reviewed this report' and 'As per my last email, here is X'.

Yawn.

Obviously, you and I have never been guilty of typing one of those phrases into an email. We are so much more interesting and creative and sparky than that. Right?

Naomi Bagdonas is a strategy and media consultant who also happens to teach humour at the Stanford Graduate School of Business and is also the co-author of the bestselling book *Humor, Seriously*. Perhaps not surprisingly, Bagdonas thinks there are a lot of benefits to injecting humour into emails.

'If we think about the barrage of electronic information we get every day, it is pretty profound,' Bagdonas explains. 'Humour is such a powerful way to separate the signal from the noise. It's a gift to someone when they read their fortieth email in the last twenty minutes and everything has been all business. And then you have this one email that has a little bit of light-heartedness. It's so incredibly powerful, whether it's a pun in the subject line, a GIF or just an unexpected line.'

Ultimately, humour is a great way to write an email that someone actually wants to respond to instead of one they will move past and de-prioritise. A funny email will also help you build stronger connections with those on the receiving end.

Bagdonas has her students carry out an email audit where they are asked to go through the last ten emails they've sent. She then runs a competition to see which student can find the most sterile business speak – a phrase that could have been written by a robot. Students share it with the class, sometimes in the chat box and other times, as a dramatic reading.

The exercise serves to remind people that the more technology-mediated our communication becomes, the easier it is to lose our sense of humour and humanity along the way. 'We subconsciously adapt for the medium. And when we're constantly communicating through technology, it's easy to sound like a robot,' she explains.

She recommends three simple ways to lighten up your emails.

First, write like a human. Instead of saying 'Please find attached the presentation slides that you requested as per our discussion', you could instead say, 'I've attached the slides for you'. While this sounds simple, it's incredibly effective – but unfortunately all too rare. Receiving an email that sounds like it is written by a real person rather than a business bot makes the message more enjoyable to read. And you don't need to be a stand-up comedian to achieve this.

Second, use what Bagdonas refers to as a serendipitous sign-off. Rather than say 'kind regards', write something relevant but unexpected. She gives an example where she started a 3 pm call and the person she was talking with mentioned how she had had three cups of coffee. Bagdonas said she was on her second cup, and they had a laugh about it. When Bagdonas signed off her post-meeting email, she said 'yours heavily caffeinated'.

Third, use callbacks. Callbacks are where you refer to a moment that already got a laugh. 'When I'm on a call, especially if it's with a new client, I will look for moments when we organically laugh together. So we're going to probably have a laugh at some point and I'll jot down that moment when they laughed and then I'll bring it back in the email. For example, I was on the phone with someone I was trying to invite to come speak at our course at Stanford. He joked that he is superstitious. And so I wrote in the email back to him: We're so hoping that you can come. We've pencilled you in while crossing our fingers, stroking rabbit-foot key chains and throwing a thousand pennies into wishing wells that you can join.'

If all else fails, Bagdonas says that a well-placed meme can be effective. Just don't overuse them. And one other word of warning when using humour: never punch down. Punching down refers to making someone of lower status than you the target of the joke. Bagdonas explained to me, 'If you are the highest person on the totem pole, or if you're in a position of authority, making fun of yourself is a really safe place to go.'

Conversely, if you are not at the top of the hierarchy in a room, feel safe 'punching up', whereby you make someone of higher status than you the target of your joke. Doing so can actually help you gain status and influence.

Put it into action

1. Conduct your own email audit. Go to your sent folder and highlight any and all jargon you have written in the last ten emails you sent.
2. Bring more levity to your emails by:
   a) Speaking like a human and avoiding business clichés.
   b) Practise using a serendipitous sign-off to end your emails on a high.
   c) Utilise callbacks, whereby you deliberately look for moments of laughter in your meetings and conversations with the email recipient and reference these in a humorous manner in your emails.
   d) Use GIFs, but sparingly.

CONNECTION
A summary

The one-page operating manual

To create your one-page operating manual, answer the following questions:

- What are your strengths? How can someone bring these out in you?
- What are your weaknesses? What tends to bring these out?
- How should people best communicate with you?
- What are your pet peeves?
- What do people misunderstand about you?

Decide how you want to share your operating manual. You could create a Word document and share it with your team and anyone new you start working with. You could even put it online for the world to see.

Communicate with your clothes

If you have an important message to communicate to your staff, think about something outside the usual communication channels that will cut through the noise. It may be your wardrobe, or with the move to more virtual meetings, perhaps your video background or a prop that you have in the background of all video calls.

The unsolicited gift

Look for opportunities to surprise people with an unsolicited gift. Instead of giving gifts at predictable times, give them when people least expect it.

Whose help do you need?

At the start of every week, clarify your priorities or goals for the week ahead. Avoid thinking of yourself as an island. Instead, ask yourself, 'Whose help do I need?' These people might be in your immediate team or outside of it. Acknowledge to yourself that it's okay to receive help to achieve your goals, as no one is expecting you to get it done on your own.

Extreme giving

When trying to build a long-term relationship with someone, adopt a mindset of generous and highly personalised giving. Keep an eye out for key milestones in that person's life, whether it be starting a new job, having a child or a big work achievement. Think about how you can support them beyond a generic email or 'like' on social media.

Reinvigorate dormant ties

Set aside time once a month (or if you want to be really ambitious like King, once a week), and write down two or three people who you haven't had contact with for a few years. Think about how you could be helpful to them. You might want to say thank you for something they did, share something with them that they might like, or even ask them for advice on something you are currently working on.

Ask about family

When trying to build a connection with someone in a professional setting, resist the urge to go straight to work-related topics. Instead, ask them about their family or their upbringing. By talking about childhood and family – experiences shared by everyone – you'll be able to build stronger and more human connections faster.

Pre-plan unique talking points

When you next have a social engagement where you don't know anyone particularly well, think about three to five things you are doing that are novel or unique. When someone asks you, as they inevitably will, 'What have you been up to?', respond with one of them.

Gamify meeting people

If you are at an event and feeling nervous, turn the experience into a game. Create a motivating reward system, such as scoring points in an imaginary game, or something tangible. Next, set yourself a goal, such as to score five points, where you receive one point per stranger you meet. Reward yourself once you hit the goal.

Look for odd numbers

Look for groups of odd-numbered people when you next find yourself at an event where you don't know anyone or you want to meet new people. Approach them and identify the person who is on the outer and try to break off into a one-on-one conversation with this person.

Send funnier emails

Conduct an email audit by opening your sent folder and highlighting all jargon you have written in the last ten emails you sent.

Bring more levity to your emails by:

a) Speaking like a human and avoiding business clichés.
b) Practise using a serendipitous sign-off to end your emails on a high.
c) Utilise callbacks, whereby you deliberately look for moments of laughter in your meetings and conversations with the email recipient and reference these in a humorous manner in your emails.
d) Use GIFs, but sparingly.

ENERGY
Maintain your spark

It's 2 pm and you're flailing. You're in the classic 'post-lunch dip' phase of the day, as psychologists call it. Even if you're still full from lunch, perhaps you gobble down some chocolate for an artificial energy boost. But sadly, you are well aware that you'll be suffering a sugar crash in twenty minutes' time.

Managing one's time can be hard enough, but often, managing energy can be even harder. Combined with our body's natural energy rhythms, we also have the fluctuations of our mood to deal with. Moreover, we can encounter unexpected stressors that have a dramatic impact on our energy. So it's time to take back control of our energy and think about the tools and techniques available to us to feel more energised more of the time. Having a full (or at least fuller) tank of energy helps us make the most of our time and thus use it more wisely.

This section starts by looking at the big picture, and how having your purpose front and centre (literally) and articulating your fulfilment factors can increase feelings of invigoration, especially when things are busy and stressful.

We will be looking at how to make hard work enjoyable and how to set the optimal pace to maintain your energy.

People who manage their energy well think deliberately about how to optimise their happiness throughout the day, and we will be looking at rituals and tricks you can adopt to make new habits stick, and experience more gratitude, humour and joy throughout the course of your day.

Finally, we will look at the things you can remove from your life to boost energy and vigour.

How a sticky note can help you be more resilient

Kate Morris had a mammoth year in 2020. Not only was she managing one of the largest online retail businesses in Australia through a pandemic, but she was also preparing to list Adore Beauty on the Australian Stock Exchange.

'I remember looking at the schedule our bankers had created,' recalls Morris. 'I said to them "There must be a mistake because you have me on back-to-back Zoom calls for twelve hours every day for several weeks". And they said, "No, that's just a standard roadshow". So I knew that for me, it wasn't about managing my time, it was about managing my energy.'

Morris discovered that the best way to manage her energy was to return to her purpose. She asked herself what she really wanted to achieve with the IPO. And the answer was clear: she wanted to be the largest ever IPO in Australia with a female founder and a female CEO. For Morris, it was about making history.

Morris's business coach encouraged her to articulate this purpose and keep it front of mind. 'So I put a little sticky note on the bottom of my computer monitor that I was going to be staring at for twelve hours a day. And the sticky note said, "Making history".

'At the start of every call, which started on the hour every hour, where I would be delivering the exact same presentation and asked the exact same questions, I would look at the sticky note. And it helped me make every presentation fresh – like it was the first time I was saying the words and answering those questions.'

In a rather unusual experiment, research led by Bruce Smith from the University of New Mexico demonstrated the power of tuning into our purpose. He found that when people were connected to what they were striving to achieve, they were able to stick their hand in very cold or very hot water for a longer period of time, compared to those who were not connected to their purpose. The researchers concluded that having a sense of purpose helps people deal with discomfort more effectively, just like how Morris dealt with the intense discomfort of twelve consecutive hours of Zoom calls day after day (arguably much less comfortable than sticking one's hand into iced water for a long period of time).

After hearing Morris share her example, I felt inspired to try it out in my own life. The thing that drives me is giving people strategies that will help them do their best work and have fun while doing it. After all, adults spend around one-third of their lives at work, so you want it to be enjoyable. So my sticky note currently reads: Help people do their best work – and have fun while doing it.

I stuck this at the bottom of my iMac, which I sit at every day. And while most days, I don't need much help feeling excited about what I do, my little note does serve as a motivating reminder on days when

I'm having trouble staying on task or working up the energy to tackle tasks I've been putting off.

Though the idea of being clear on your purpose is nothing new, for me, the big difference is the simplicity of having a sticky note stuck on my computer that acts as a constant, daily reminder of why I choose to spend my time in a particular way.

Put it into action

1. Think about the main motivator that drives you to do your work every day. It might be specific to a big project you are working on or it might be something that relates to your career more generally.
2. Try to express this reason, or purpose, in a short phrase or sentence.
3. Write it down and stick it somewhere where you work so you will see it every day.
4. If your purpose changes, or if you finish up the big project that your purpose related to, freshen it up with something new and more relevant.

An easy way to track
if things are going off-track

Cast your mind back to the last really crappy day that you had. You might have woken up feeling groggy after a bad night's sleep, had a day full of meetings, felt like you were constantly running behind schedule, and not finished work in time to have dinner with your family. It was probably a day when you felt the opposite of fulfilled.

Leadership and motivation writer and consultant Dr Jason Fox became hyper aware of days that lacked fulfilment. 'I know there's a spiral that happens for me when I'm travelling a lot interstate or internationally for work with clients,' describes Fox. 'The flights, the time difference, the diet that changes when I'm in hotels, the sleeping in different rooms. It can set me on this spiral in terms of health and making bad choices.

'I also know that if I have more than three days pass where I haven't done my morning journaling or my morning ritual, that's usually an early indicator that something's going on here. And if more than three days pass when I haven't had time to read books or feed my curiosity, that's also an early warning sign.'

For Fox, these are warning signs of not prioritising what he calls fulfilment factors. Several years ago, Fox and his partner sat down to identify a list of around five factors that were personally important to leading a fulfilling life. They looked at things they found frustrating and thought about what the opposites were. And they also thought about what brought them joy and made them feel in flow.

As an example, healthiness is one of Fox's most valued fulfilment factors. To break the abstract down into something measurable, Fox sets himself markers to track whether he is prioritising this fulfilment factor. This means going to the gym three times a week and getting seven hours sleep every night.

Another fulfilment factor for Fox is curiosity. This means prioritising a certain number of hours in his week to read and learn and reflect.

To keep his fulfilment factors front of mind, Fox and his partner have a calendar poster stuck on the wall of their home office where they mark off when they are doing activities that relate to their fulfilment factors. Fox previously had tracked activities digitally, but he found it was too easy to forget about them when they were hidden away in an online folder.

The calendar gives Fox a visual representation of ensuring he is living a life in line with his fulfilment factors, and shows him, at a glance, when circumstances are out of whack and need to be adjusted. Feeling responsible for one's time in this way, and giving oneself the opportunity to wrestle back control from all the things that make us busy, empowers us to live a more fulfilled life and one where we are using our time and energy wisely.

Put it into action

1. Make a list of things that really frustrate you. For example, finishing work late and not getting to spend enough time with your partner or kids in the evening might be a constant source of frustration. Next, think about why this is so frustrating. For example, it could mean that time with family is a priority for you, and so it's frustrating when work cuts into this time.
2. Now do the opposite: make a list of things that bring you joy, make you feel energised or get you in flow. This might include different professional and recreational activities,

types of interactions or pursuits relating to people in your life, and of course, your physical and mental health.

3. Look for themes emerging from these lists. Some example themes that people often gravitate towards include health, family, friends, learning, sport, personal development, craft, making things and writing.

4. Prioritise your list to select the three to five most important.

5. Think about measurable activities that relate to your fulfilment factors. For example, if friendship is one of your factors, a measurable activity might be catching up with at least one friend for a meal or walk every week.

6. Track your activities and do a weekly or monthly check-in with yourself to ensure that you are prioritising your fulfilment factors in your life.

How to make
hard work enjoyable

A false dichotomy exists in the world of work: we are led to believe that deep, focused work should feel hard. That there's no gain without pain. We need to feel as if we struggled through something in order to feel as though we achieved a worthwhile outcome. Like writing this book: the more I complain to friends about how earth-shatteringly challenging and exhausting writing a manuscript is, the better the book will be. Right?

Critically acclaimed author of *Essentialism* and *Effortless*, Greg McKeown, thinks this is nonsense. There is nothing stopping us from making hard work also feel enjoyable.

McKeown used to really dislike making lots of phone calls for work. They were the one aspect of his job that felt like drudgery. So he experimented with a ritual he learned from another entrepreneur to make this activity fun.

'If I have a lot of phone calls to make, I sit in the hot tub. And I tell people where I am calling them from – it's not a secret. We just laugh about it and we still get the job done. But it's a more enjoyable environment.'

McKeown believes this can be achieved with just about any activity in life. 'There's nothing written that says essential things must be hard. And yet lots of people believe exactly that: if it's not drudgery, it can't be important work.'

He also applies this strategy to his home life. 'My family has rituals around eating together. We'll toast each other at the beginning of

the meal sometimes, or we'll do shout-outs for what's gone right. But then after dinner, my children are like ninjas. Not only do they just disappear, they do it silently. And they've all got very good excuses once I try to play the cat-and-mouse game of getting them back to the kitchen to help with clean-up.'

McKeown thought about how he could make clean-up enjoyable. The solution came in the form of Disney music. McKeown's eldest daughter loves singing Disney tunes. So to turn what felt like hard work into fun, McKeown started playing Disney classics during clean-up time. And now, his family genuinely enjoys the cleaning-up ritual because the music and dancing and singing that is part of the process makes it fun and energising.

Put it into action

1. Think about a type of work that you do regularly – or even something that you do in your home life – that feels like drudgery. Perhaps it's emails, phone calls, household chores or ploughing through a huge project that you're currently working on.

2. Next, think about something you really enjoy that you could pair with this activity. Could you listen to your favourite music while replying to email? Do you have a hot tub, like McKeown, or simply an outdoor space with a nice view, where you could make phone calls from?

3. Start to consistently pair the hard work with something that makes it more enjoyable. If you do this often enough, you may actually start to look forward to the activity that once felt as if it was sucking the life out of you.

The optimal pace
for hard work

When Greg McKeown was working on his second bestselling book, *Effortless*, he reflected a lot on his process for writing it. 'There were some things that I did that made it a lot harder than it needed to be, such as any day that I worked beyond about three hours,' McKeown told me.

'If I tried to do four hours or six hours or longer, I didn't just hit diminishing returns, I'd hit negative returns. Diminishing returns is where for every unit of effort you put in, you're getting a little less. But negative returns are for every unit of effort you're putting in, you're actually getting a worse overall result.'

On the days when McKeown put in more than four hours' work, he felt as though the manuscript was ending up worse than it had been before he started that day. He learned that he needed to get the pace right. So he trialled a different strategy to approach writing the book.

'I said to myself: every day I'm going to work on the manuscript and open the Google document. That's my minimum standard. I will go into it. But the maximum amount of work I will do will never be more than three hours.'

He essentially set upper and lower bounds for what he would accomplish every day. He also thought about the upper and lower bounds for how many words he would write each day.

'You're trying to make sure that you don't use up more mental energy than you can recuperate each day and each week. You want to be able to sustain the pace and get the job done. This is in contrast to being intermittent in your effort where you go big for a couple of days and then you can't even work on it after that because you fried your brain, and you can't get back to it.'

Professor Maura Scott led research that demonstrated the impact of setting upper and lower bounds. She asked a group of people to set a goal for weight loss, such as to lose two kilograms. Meanwhile, other participants were told to set a range, such as losing between one and three kilograms. Those who set a range instead of a specific number were more likely to lose weight. Scott suggested this was because the lower bound felt more attainable, which led to a sense of confidence and determination, while the upper bound felt inspiring and ambitious, leading to feelings of hope and optimism.

I thought about this strategy a lot when I was writing this book. When I was working on the first draft, I ideally wanted to write two sections per day – about 1000–1200 words. But I had a lower bound of writing just one section and an upper bound of writing three. Given I have a tendency to constantly try to beat my own goals (could I write ten sections in a day?), pacing myself meant that I was able to sustain a steady pace during the writing process and never get close to burning out. I was also able to submit the manuscript early.

Put it into action

1. Think about a big project you are currently working on.
2. Working backwards from your deadline, set yourself an upper and lower bound for how much you need to accomplish each day to meet your deadline.
3. Ideally frame the upper and lower bounds as output as opposed to hours spent working on the task, as it's ultimately your output (not hours) that will get you closer to your end target.

How to make a habit actually stick

You might have heard that it takes twenty-one days to create a new habit. Or perhaps you heard it takes sixty-six days. Or maybe as short as two weeks. Unfortunately, these are all mistruths about habit formation. It turns out that repetition is not the key to success when trying to make new habits stick. While the strength of a new habit may be correlated with repetition, it doesn't actually cause it.

B.J. Fogg is an experimental psychologist who founded and directs the Behaviour Design Lab at Stanford University and is the author of the bestseller *Tiny Habits*. Fogg has found that the key to behaviour change is to create Tiny Habits. These are behaviours that you do at least once a day, take no more than thirty seconds and require little effort.

He says that to make a new behaviour stick, you need to boil it down so it's tiny. 'So instead of doing twenty push-ups, you just do two,' he explained to me on *How I Work*. 'Instead of flossing all your teeth, you do just one. Instead of reading a whole chapter, just read a sentence.'

The next step is to figure out where in your life the new habit will naturally fit. For example, after you brush your teeth, you might floss one – if flossing is the habit you are trying to form. As you sip your morning coffee, you might read one sentence (and yes, this might feel strange) if you are trying to build in more reading to your day.

The crux of making the habit stick is a technique Fogg calls 'celebration', where you do something that causes a positive emotion inside yourself. Fogg says it is emotion that creates new habits.

'For me, one that works is I do a double fist pump and go "awesome". By doing that, it signals to your brain that this is success and then your brain starts making that a habit. You're hacking your brain through celebrations.'

When you supercharge habit formation by celebrating the new behaviour, or even just creating a positive feeling, you will naturally start to extend the behaviour. After getting into the habit of flossing one tooth, you will eventually floss them all (much to your dentist's delight). Or by doing two push-ups, you'll naturally want to continue and work your way up to a much larger number.

Taking the impact of positive emotion on behaviour change a step further, Fogg gave me an example of something as simple as writing with a certain pen. 'I've got a pen sitting in front of me, and it's purple. I pick up this pen and I start writing with it and I'm like, "Oh my gosh, my handwriting is neater and the pen is smoother on the paper and I feel so successful using this purple pen".

'Well guess what? This afternoon when I come to write a note to my mum or something like that and I have all these pens in front of me, I'll reach for the purple pen because that's the one that made me feel successful. And if that feeling is strong enough and clear enough and if my brain associates this feeling of great handwriting, then I'm not going to be reaching for the blue pen or the black pen or the red pen any time soon. I'm just going to always go back to the purple pen.'

Fogg calls this an instant habit. Instant habits form when we do things once, it feels good, and then we stop considering the alternatives. Reflecting on my own life, I can identify a number of instant habits. I have a particular chair at home that unconsciously became my reading chair. It's positioned away from any technology and feels so comfortable to sit in (it looks pretty cute too since I had it reupholstered in a dusty pink) and as a result, I power through books when sitting in this chair. And now, it's literally the only chair in my house in which I read, despite there being several other comfortable chairs and couches in my home.

Put it into action

1. Think about a new habit you want to create. It might be around work, family, health or something else entirely.
2. Break down the new habit into its tiniest step. For example, you might want to start a regular meditation practice. The tiny version of that new habit (something you can do in 30 seconds or less) might be taking three deep breaths.
3. Link that new habit with something you currently do every day, such as going to bed at night. Say to yourself, 'When my head hits the pillow at night, I will take three deep breaths'.
4. Finally, celebrate the behaviour. You might do a fist pump like Fogg does or yell, 'I am a habit-forming legend!' or something else that feels good and creates positive emotion. By linking the new behaviour with a positive emotion, it will start to become automatic.
5. You might also want to become mindful of instant habits. These almost work in reverse to the tiny habits that you deliberately create. Become conscious of new behaviours you're adopting and reflect on whether they are serving you. You will probably find they became an instant habit because they produced a positive feedback loop. But if the behaviour is unproductive, consider applying the Tiny Habit theory to adjust the behaviour into something that is productive and enriching for your life.

Why you need to make a joke of serious work

When seventeen- to twenty-year-olds were asked by Gallup in 2013 if they smiled or laughed a lot yesterday, 85 per cent said 'yes'. This figure drops to 60 per cent when we hit our mid-twenties, right when most of us are entering the workforce.

We are taught that work is serious – and serious things don't mix with humour or levity. But in fact, research suggests that bringing humour into the office will significantly improve our work. And that's not a joke.

Strategy and media consultant Naomi Bagdonas and Professor Jennifer Aaker teach humour at Stanford Graduate School of Business and are authors of the book *Humor, Seriously*. While Aaker had written books beforehand, it was Bagdonas's first one. Aaker warned Bagdonas how difficult writing a book would be. 'It's harder than you think,' she told her co-writer when they first agreed to collaborate. (FYI, Naomi, I concur.)

'So from the beginning, we tried to set up these hacks that would remind us not to take the work or ourselves too seriously,' Bagdonas told me.

One way the authors did this was to lower expectations, especially for their first draft. Bagdonas described writing the first words of a book as being really intimidating. 'So, instead of creating a document with a manuscript title and all of the formal stuff, we just created a Google Document and called it Words on a Page.'

'The goal was just to lower the bar. It's like, "We're not writing a book. We're just putting down some words on a page. That's all we're here to do.'" Adopting this mindset and lowering expectations right down made it far easier to get started with the writing process.

The pair used this strategy again when it came time to writing a book proposal. A book proposal document can be a scary thing to create. It's like a long and detailed business plan, but for a book. And it's the document that publishers use to assess whether they will buy and publish your magnum opus.

Using a similar strategy, the authors avoided calling the document a 'book proposal'. Instead, they created another Google Doc and titled it A Really Shitty Proposal.

'So every time we opened this doc, it would say our Really Shitty Proposal. And I'd text Jennifer at 6 am and say, "Hey, I'm in the shitty proposal right now. I'll see you there later today".'

The document name stuck, but then the authors accidentally sent it to a publisher without changing the title. Perhaps not surprisingly, the publishers loved it and so Bagdonas and Aaker ended up pitching it to all publishers as A Really Shitty Proposal. And the rest, as they say, is history (or more specifically, a book that turned into a national bestseller).

Put it into action

1. The next time you have a really big, challenging task, think about how you can incorporate some humour or levity into the process to make it more energising.
2. You might want to do what Bagdonas and Aaker did and give the project a humorous name. You might want to use visual humour by inserting a funny meme into the opening page of a report that you are working on every day. Or perhaps you might want to invite your project team to kick off all meetings with some 80s music. Because 80s music makes everything better.

Why you need
a Spark Joy folder

When I was completing my Doctorate in Organisational Psychology, I concurrently pursued a side hustle (albeit one that generated very little income) as a musician. I had recorded a ten-track album with a producer and was shopping it around to record labels. Chasing a career where rejection is the norm can be hard, so I set myself the goal of not expecting to receive any kind of positive response until I had received enough rejection letters to cover one entire wall of my bedroom. Due to the insane amount of talent I possessed (kidding – luck was clearly on my side), I only had to receive a dozen rejection letters before being offered a record deal. Barely enough to cover a corner of my bedroom wall.

We all receive professional rejections. If you work in a creative industry, you may experience rejection more than most. But even if you work in a 'standard' office job, rejections can still be uncomfortably frequent. You are knocked back for a promotion. You receive a less-than-glowing performance review. You're not invited to join a project team that you were really keen to be a part of (don't worry – you were better off without them. Trust me).

Scott Sonenshein is a bestselling author (he's the co-author, with Marie Kondo, of *Joy at Work*) and Professor of Management at Rice University. He is also someone who chose a career where criticism is frequently dished out. 'We are criticised and receive feedback when we submit manuscripts,' he explains. 'We have these anonymous reviewers who are telling us how bad our work is, even if it eventually gets published. We receive criticisms on our teaching evaluations. And because bad information is more salient and feels more real than good information – such as the one bad comment on your teaching evaluation – you're always going to remember that.'

Our overemphasis on the negative has a name: Negativity Bias. It's our propensity to place more emphasis on negative information and stimuli compared to positive. Humans are basically suckers for punishment. While Sonenshein acknowledges that criticism is important and it's what leads to growth, too much of it can be overwhelming. 'Let's face it: it's emotionally exhausting to be constantly told "Do this better or do that better".'

To overcome this bias, he wanted to find a way of reminding himself of all the joy he received from his work, especially when faced with a barrage of negative feedback or criticism. So he created a folder on his desktop called the Spark Joy folder.

'I'll put a rotating bunch of items that spark joy in it. It could be a family photo, it could be a paper I recently published, or a comment from a speaking host that gave me praise on something I did, or a positive teaching evaluation. I'll go into that folder usually at least once a day and just read a couple things. It helps me feel good about

one of the things that I've been able to do.' And when it comes to using your time wisely, a Spark Joy folder will help set you back on track if you're feeling demotivated, by reminding you of your strengths and greater purpose.

Put it into action

1. Think about what your version of a Spark Joy folder looks like. It might be digital, like Sonenshein's, or it might be analogue, such as having a box or an actual cardboard folder on your desk.
2. Dig out some artefacts that spark joy for you. These might be photos, emails, feedback you've received, accomplishments (e.g. a certificate) or something else entirely.
3. Pop these artefacts into your Spark Joy folder.
4. Moving forward, whenever you receive something that makes you feel happy, move it to your Spark Joy folder.
5. As you collect more artefacts that spark joy, consider archiving some of the contents of your folder so you keep your Spark Joy folder fresh.

How your computer password can make you more productive

Decades of research has shown that gratitude makes us feel good. For example, Robert Emmons from the University of California, Davis, found that people who kept a daily or weekly gratitude journal for ten weeks were significantly happier than those who wrote about neutral or negative life events. Other research found that teenagers who were asked to think about things they were grateful for reported significantly higher life satisfaction than those who thought about hassles or neutral events. And this effect lasted for three weeks after the experiment.

So we all know gratitude is good, and gratitude journals are particularly good. But do you keep one? Me neither. But don't worry, because we're in good company. Bestselling author and happiness guru Gretchen Rubin found that the practice of keeping a gratitude journal simply didn't work for her. Instead of finding the exercise helpful, she found it annoying, and the habit never stuck.

However, as someone who has dedicated more than a decade of her life to studying happiness, she was determined to find another method for feeling grateful and not taking the good things in her life for granted. Rather than forcing herself to sit down and reflect on what she was grateful for every single day, she thought about linking gratitude to some of her daily behaviours.

Rubin lives in an apartment building in New York City. There are two doors she has to walk through to get in and out of her building, which she goes through every day. 'I always try to use those doors as a transition point. When I walk out, I think to myself how happy I am to be going out into New York city, my favourite city. And then when I walk through the doors at the end of the day to go home, I think to myself how happy I am to be coming home to my cosy apartment.

'The forced pause of going through those two doors acts as a way to remind myself to be grateful.'

She has heard people describe other everyday activities they undertake that constitute a version of gratitude practice. For example, some of her readers were using something they were grateful for as the password to their computer. Others had saved photos of gratitudes as a screensaver or lock screen image on their phone.

Incorporating reminders of what you are grateful for into actions you undertake on a daily basis and without thinking, such as entering passwords or unlocking your phone, makes it almost effortless to sustain a gratitude practice. It also happens to be a very time-efficient way to bake gratitude into your day. And given gratitude leads to happiness and happy people achieve more, your computer password can now have the potential to boost your productivity.

Put it into action

1. Think of something you do every day. It might be one of the behaviours mentioned above such as entering your password into your computer or walking through your front door. It might be getting into your car or brushing your teeth.
2. Start small and decide what one thing you want to be more consciously grateful for in your life.
3. Consider how you will link this gratitude to your chosen behaviour. It might be as simple as thinking about the thing you are grateful for whenever you undertake the behaviour. Or you might incorporate it in a written form, such as composing a note to yourself that expresses the gratitude and saving a picture of that note on the lock screen of your phone.

4. Start to link other things you are grateful for to other daily behaviours until they, too, become integrated into your day-to-day life.

5. If you want to broaden your focus of what you appreciate in life, then feel free to add and subtract the things you acknowledge in this way.

It's time to
stop rushing

Some days, I feel as if my default state is 'rushed'. I am rushing to complete tasks, rushing to get to a meeting on time, rushing to scoff down my lunch. Feeling rushed is a pretty unpleasant feeling – it's like having an angry cloud of stress following you around for the entire day. But when I stop to reflect on what is causing me to feel so rushed, it's simply down to my own unrealistic expectations.

I often meet external deadlines way ahead of time, but when I impose my own internal deadlines, I feel rushed – it's like a self-inflicted sense of pressure. I hate nothing more than being late to a meeting. I work myself into a stress if I am even running just a couple of minutes late: God forbid the person I am meeting with be kept waiting for sixty seconds. And because of my need for efficiency, I often pack my day tightly with tasks I want to accomplish and meetings to attend, leaving little room for buffer.

Feeling rushed is exhausting. I'm yawning just writing about it. But when I interviewed comedian Meshel Laurie, she had an antidote to my rushed-ness.

Laurie discovered Buddhism more than a decade ago. One of the teachings she follows is to let other people go first, in every way. 'In traffic, when you're walking through doors, when you're getting on an escalator, when you're getting in the lift,' describes Laurie. 'Just the simple act of standing back and gesturing for other people to go in front of you is a really great exercise in humility.'

Through getting into the habit of always letting others go first,

Laurie has noticed that it is a great way to make other people happy. And while she admits it can be a tricky habit to consistently maintain, it's a great intention to run your day with.

For Laurie, driving on busy streets is a great way to practise letting others go first. 'We're all in traffic all the time and you start to think to yourself "Why am I such a tight-arse in traffic? Why am I pretending I'm not seeing that person who's trying to get in here? Why don't I just let them in?" It's going to only be an extra five minutes for me. And so I let people in. And it's so massive to them.'

Laurie was recently interviewing a brain surgeon for her podcast *Calm Ya Farm*. She often says to people, 'Who cares if you're running late – no one's going to die'. 'Well, if this brain surgeon was running late, someone might die. But for the rest of us, if we are late for work, no one is going to die.'

I need to remind myself of this fact the next time I am stressing about running one minute late to a meeting. Because if we can have a healthier perspective of time and avoid wasting precious energy on being a few minutes late, we will save that energy for more important tasks and activities.

Put it into action

1. In the morning, set an intention for the day to let others go first.
2. You might want to start slowly and simply practise letting others go first in traffic. Once you get the hang of that, let others go first in a queue or through a door. And then take it to interactions you have with people and let others go first in a meeting, for example, to give their point of view before you speak.

Why it's worth considering buying more time

I am a big vegetable eater, as is my daughter. Between us, we would easily eat ten serves or more per day. We used to have a weekly ritual where we would head to an inner-city market in Melbourne and buy a week's supply every Saturday. I would then spend several hours on Saturday afternoon doing food prep in the form of washing, cutting and packing around fifteen Tupperware containers full of vegetables. While I loved the feeling of a fridge full of prepared, healthy food, I hated the hours I dedicated to this mind-numbing task week after week, which I wasn't even particularly good at (my knife skills leave much to be desired).

My (now ex-) husband made a suggestion one weekend: Why didn't I post an ad on Airtasker and see if I could find someone to cut vegetables for me? This was a revelation. Could I simply use money to remove this annoying weekly task from my life permanently? Oh yes, I could.

I found a university student who worked part-time in a cafe doing food preparation. She came to my house for two hours every week to prepare the weeks' worth of vegetables and I paid her $50. This was hands-down the best $50 I spent during my week. This $50 bought me so much joy, as I won back several hours every weekend that I could spend outside of the kitchen and doing something fun with my family instead. (And let me also acknowledge that I am lucky to have $50 to dedicate to slicing and dicing cucumbers and carrots, as not everyone is in this position.)

Psychology Professor Elizabeth Dunn was not surprised when I shared this anecdote with her. 'We published a series of eight studies in one of the leading scientific journals demonstrating that people who use money to buy time are happier than those who don't.

'I've definitely struggled with this fundamental dilemma that I think so many of us face these days, which is there's so much more to do than I have time to do,' she told me.

In her household, cleaning is a source of disagreement. Dunn was lucky enough to marry someone who is a really good cleaner, unlike herself. 'My husband just marvels at the amount of time it takes me to clean up our teeny-tiny kitchen. So I've always been in favour of paying somebody to come in and help with the cleaning each week. And he has always disagreed with me on that,' she said with a laugh.

Dunn ended up winning the 'fight' and now they have a wonderful friend of the family who comes in every week to clean for a few hours. It's been a win for the marriage and personally for Dunn. 'I no longer have to devote my whole Saturday afternoon to try and make our house not be a complete disaster.'

Put it into action

1. Make a list of the tasks that drain you of energy or time, or ideally, both. These might be tasks you have to do at work or at home, such as repetitive administrative tasks, chores or even things that you are not very good at, as in the case of Dunn and cleaning.
2. Pick the task that takes up the most time per week and investigate how much it would cost to pay someone else to do it. For example, administrative tasks can be outsourced to a virtual assistant, generally at the cost of $5–10 per hour. Household chores can often be outsourced for between $20–40 per hour.
3. Run an experiment where you pay someone to do this task for four weeks. At the end of the experiment, reflect on how

eliminating the task from your life has made you feel, how much time it has freed up, and whether it therefore feels like a good financial investment. If it does, keep doing it! If not, work down your task list and experiment with other tasks you could pay someone to do that will free up time in your life.

How to remove recurring irritants from your life

Bestselling author Dan Heath told me that he often wakes up in an irritable mood. To make matters worse, at the time he had a human alarm clock in the form of a sixteen-month-old toddler. Whenever it was Heath's turn to wake up with his daughter, he would get dressed in the dark to avoid disturbing his wife. If you've ever tried to get dressed in the dark, you'll appreciate that this is not easy.

Putting his shirt on proved to be a recurring challenge. 'Is it inside out? Is it right side out? I can't see the tag in the dark. I can't see the letters on the front of the shirt in the dark,' he said. 'And so I'm just taking a stab and for some reason, my experience is that nine times out of ten I guess wrong, and then I'm kind of irritated.'

The situation Heath described is a classic example of a recurring irritant: a regular annoyance in one's life.

In his bestselling book *Upstream*, Heath wrote about another recurring irritant that I could relate to. He described how he does his best writing from a cafe. He sits at the same table, puts on his headphones and immediately gets to work. But part of this ritual involves lugging his laptop around and so, every time he goes to the cafe, he has to fish his power cord out of the bag, plug it into the wall, and then when he gets back to his office, he has to dig the power cord out of the bag again and plug it in the wall.

'I've got a hundred cords around my desk. So it's always just a little bit of a nuisance. But this just seemed like that's the way it has to be,' Heath explained.

In the process of writing *Upstream* and thinking about solving problems closer to their root cause, it occurred to Heath that he could actually live in a world where he had two power cords. So he bought a second one which lives in his laptop bag. Genius. (He also started laying out his clothes the night before.)

So why did it take Heath writing a book on problem solving to identify this simple solution for his own life?

It was because of a force called Tunnelling. Tunnelling was coined by Princeton University Psychology Professor Eldar Shafir and Chicago Booth Economist Sendhil Mullainathan. When we have limited cognitive resources (i.e. brain power) due to life stresses, our brain adopts tunnel vision and misses the opportunity to identify and solve problems. And when we are dealing with one or two big issues in our lives, our brain power diminishes further so we don't have the mental capacity to deal with other demands.

In the context of problem solving, when we have a few really big issues to fix, we simply don't have the resources or ability to resolve every single predicament (especially the little ones). We adopt tunnel vision and, as a result, engage in short-term, reactive thinking – which is why Heath failed to stop and think about how best to solve his power cord and T-shirt problems, and instead, put up with them. Indeed, research has shown that our IQ drops by ten points when we have a big problem overriding our thinking, compared to when the big problem is absent. (If you think about what the pandemic did to our brains, it probably made us all a bit stupider.)

How do you escape Tunnelling? You need to give yourself some slack, in the form of time or resources. And finding and eliminating recurring irritants will help you free up time and energy in your life.

Put it into action

1. Make a list of recurring irritants in your life. These are tasks that you do regularly that frustrate you, annoy you or you

simply find boring. Ideally, pick tasks you do regularly –
once a week or even daily.

2. To uncover more recurring irritants, ask a co-worker or
family member what they observe you doing that you
shouldn't, what is a poor use of your time and what gets you
frustrated.

3. Start to find solutions in one of four ways:
   - Delegate it. Consider delegating the recurring irritant to
     another team member or use some hired help via websites
     such as Upwork.com or Airtasker.com.
   - Stop doing it. Your recurring irritant may be a report
     that nobody reads or attending a meeting to which you
     don't add much value. Stop doing it and see if anything
     negative happens. It may come as a surprise that no one
     may even notice.
   - Purchase or create a solution. It could be as simple as
     an additional power cord for your laptop. If the cost out-
     weighs the irritation, purchase or create a solution.
   - Alter the activity so that it's no longer irritating. Pair the
     task with something you enjoy.

4. Download a worksheet to help identify and remove your
   recurring irritants at amantha.com/timewise

A guilt-free way
to say 'no'

I once read that the most effective productivity tip is to simply say 'no'. By saying 'no', we avoid spreading ourselves too thin and can focus on the things that matter most.

Unfortunately, saying 'no' more often is easier said than done. Particularly if you are a people-pleaser (like me), or someone who genuinely wants to help others as much as possible (yep, that's me too), saying 'no' can be hard and feel awful.

But here's the thing: the busier you are and the more successful you become in your career, the more requests you will have for your time. Which is where learning to say 'no' becomes even more important.

Mia Freedman receives a lot of requests. As the co-founder and Chief Creative Officer of the Mamamia women's media company in Australia, and the host of two podcasts (one of them daily), she is an insanely busy woman.

Freedman used to be terrible at saying 'no'. 'Like most women, I wanted people to like me and I wanted to not disappoint anybody. And so what I would do is because I didn't want to make someone feel bad for the ten seconds that it would take them to read that I was turning down whatever they wanted me to do, I would say "okay" just to put that off. But then what I would do is buy a whole problem for Future Me, which was I've promised to go to Brisbane, or do this speech, or go somewhere after work. And then that time would come around and I would really not want to do it. And it would really take a toll on me and my family.'

So Freedman found a strategy to help make saying 'no' much easier. She started to set rules for herself and change the language she used when responding to requests.

'Instead of saying "I can't" I say "I don't". It sounds really subtle but it's really important. I have rules like: I don't do black tie functions. I don't do lunches during the week. I don't do premiers. I don't do speaking or charity engagements on weekends.'

By having strict and clear rules and using the language of 'don't', it takes the 'Should I? Should I not?' out of the equation. And for Freedman, having clear and concrete rules helps her in all aspects of life.

'I exercise every day because that's easier than exercising two or three times a week. It's less mental stress on me because it's just a non-negotiable. It's like cleaning your teeth. Imagine if you only had to clean your teeth two or three days a week. And then every night you'd go, "Should it have been tonight? Oh, I don't know. But then tomorrow night I'm going to be tired because I've got that thing on. And I don't know." That part of your brain doesn't have to think, "Should I brush my teeth tonight or not," because you brush your teeth every day.

'I'm one of those people that needs hard and fast rules. Otherwise, I find myself negotiating with myself. And that's exhausting.'

She also found that when she started using the language of 'I don't' in response to requests on her time, people stopped trying to argue with her or talk her into what they wanted from her.

'When you say, "I don't do lunches," that's very clear. But if you say, "I can't have lunch on Tuesday" the person might then say, "What about Wednesday?" And it's like, "How about never? Is never good for you?"' she jokes. 'It's a clear line in the sand.'

Freedman does two other things when saying no.

'I'm very honest. I say, "Thanks so much for the invitation but the demands of running a business and having a young family means that I just can't do anything except those two things." And no one can argue when you say work and family. No one can go, "Aw, but please?"'

She also responds quickly.

'People are incredibly appreciative if you respond quickly. Because what most people do is think, "Oh, I don't want to disappoint them so I'll just ignore that." But people don't mind hearing "no". They'd prefer a "yes" but they'll deal with a "no".' And removing the anguish of worrying about disappointing people with this strategy means that you remain the boss of your time and energy.

Put it into action

1. Think about what your rules are when it comes to what you don't want to do. Write them down, beginning with the words 'I don't'. For example, I receive several guest pitches every day for *How I Work*. To make quicker decisions, I have rules that I apply to make those decisions speedy and straightforward.
2. When someone makes a request of you that breaks one of your rules, say 'no' by using the phrase 'I don't do X'.
3. Say 'no' quickly. While this may feel uncomfortable at first, you'll quickly find that people appreciate it. For me, I try to say 'no' to requests within twenty-four hours. I have done this literally hundreds of times and often, I receive an appreciative response from the person I said 'no' to.
4. Just be honest. It's hard for people to argue with honesty.

The power of 'Yes, but'

Productivity 'gurus' love talking about the power of saying 'no'. But if you operate from a mindset of generosity, as many successful leaders do, saying 'no' all the time can start to feel a bit rubbish, not to mention misaligned with your values.

Nicky Sparshott has not one, but two CEO roles. She is the Global CEO of luxury tea retailer T2 and the CEO of Unilever Australia and New Zealand. Perhaps not surprisingly, she says 'no' quite a bit. And she is a fan of giving a fast 'no' so that people can make alternate arrangements. But she is also mindful of keeping her 'no's to a minimum.

'"No" is a really important word, but depending on how it's used, it can shut down conversations before they've even had the opportunity to start,' Sparshott explains. 'There is something about "yes" that just gives the room for possibility and options. And quite often, I've been in groups and there has been a naysayer that's constantly saying "No, it can't be done. No, we've tried it before. No, it will never work."' While she acknowledges that someone playing devil's advocate is a valuable thing, you always need a few people in the room to ask what's possible.

Sparshott's secret is in how to say 'yes', but without overcommitting herself. So her go-to answer has become, 'Yes, but'.

'Yes, but I won't be able to do it for another six months. Yes, but I'll only be able to give you twenty minutes of my time at this stage. Yes, I would love to be able to participate, but I can't be there in person – could I drop you an email with my thoughts instead? It's about finding ways that allow you to share even just a little, but in a way that's reflective of the time that you have. So that's something that I try to do as much as I can.'

Interestingly, research has shown that people tend to value and appreciate small acts of kindness more than anticipated. In one study published in the *Journal of Personality and Social Psychology*, people had to recall times in their past where someone had been kind to them and reflect on how grateful they felt. The researchers found the degree to which they felt grateful was not strongly related to the amount of money or time the other person spent. Instead, their level of gratitude was more related to whether the act was useful or not.

'There are some instances where I know that I can't necessarily add value, nor would it be a great use of my time, but I typically try to allocate a little bit of my time in a purposeful way,' says Sparshott. 'I'm making sure I do have a bit of time to give when people ask for help, in large part because I have been so fortunate to have people that have done that for me in my career.' So without having to surrender huge amounts of time, you can make valuable, albeit small, contributions and pay good deeds forward.

Put it into action

1. The next time you have a request made on your time, pause before saying a blanket 'yes' or 'no'.
2. Instead, look for middle ground. Is there a way that you can help a bit, without overcommitting yourself?
3. Frame your response as 'Yes, but . . .', outlining the constraints that you are placing on your 'yes'. By doing this, you'll be able to be generous in your giving, but also uphold boundaries on your time.

Create a
to-don't list

To-do lists are considered very sexy in productivity circles (I personally find them incredibly attractive). And this book has covered several different ways to make to-do lists work harder for you. But have you ever thought about writing a list of things that you *don't* want to do?

Rachel Botsman is a world-renowned expert on trust and technology and a Trust Fellow at Oxford University. Prior to the pandemic, Botsman had written an annual 'to-don't list' for several years. The purpose of this list had been to reflect on habits she wanted to break or things she wanted to do differently. But during her first COVID lockdown, she took this ritual and made it monthly.

'I think the trigger was not travelling and realising how much I didn't want to go back to it,' Botsman explained. 'So much of our lives are programmed to "add" tasks and commitments – we're not taught how to subtract.'

She felt as though her work was constantly about adding tasks and responsibilities. To counter this feeling of the never-ending list of things to do, she diaries an appointment with herself on the last Friday of every month where she sets aside time to consider what she wants to stop doing in her work.

'I give myself a full hour to think about it and reflect on the last month's list. What did I keep? What did I find hard? Why? What is a pattern I can't break?'

While there aren't specific categories she thinks about in relation to what she wants to not do, she does think about her energy. During her meeting with herself, she reflects on how she spends her time, who she spends it with, and what she wants to focus on – and more importantly, not focus on.

Some examples of items that have made Botsman's to-don't list include:

- Don't work with clients whose intentions/motives are not aligned with yours.
- Don't undervalue things you find super easy.
- Don't schedule meetings between 8 and 11 am.
- Don't scroll through social media after 7 pm.
- Don't bend to other people's agendas.
- Don't see X person, period (!).
- Don't do 'favours' because you feel bad.

For Botsman, the process has been immensely beneficial in helping her be more mindful about where she puts her energy and helps her think about old things in new ways. And through avoiding the temptation to constantly add things to her plate, it's also helped her stay focused on the work that matters to her most.

Put it into action

1. Diarise a meeting with yourself once a month. Label it your 'To-Don't' meeting.
2. Reflect on the month that has just gone and ask yourself what de-energised or deflated you most during this period in both your personal and professional life. You might consider daily habits (such as checking social media), people you saw (who perhaps felt like human Dementors, sucking the life out of you), or things you said 'yes' to but later regretted.
3. Create a list of things you will not do the following month. Keep this list in eyesight of your desk to act as a constant reminder.

4. In subsequent months, review how you went sticking to your to-don't list, what served you and what didn't. Add or subtract items based on your reflections of what and who sucked up your energy and could thus benefit from being removed from the following month.

ENERGY
A summary

Purpose on a sticky note

Think about the main reason that drives you to do your work every day. Express this reason, or purpose, in a short phrase or sentence. Write it down and stick it somewhere where you work so you will see it every day.

Track fulfilment factors

Make a list of activities that really frustrate you and reflect on why they are so frustrating. Then, do the opposite: make a list of experiences that bring you joy or make you feel energised or get you in flow.

Look for themes emerging from these lists. Use these themes to identify and prioritise your fulfilment factors. Think about measurable activities that relate to your main fulfilment factors. Track your activities and do a weekly or monthly check-in with yourself to ensure that you are prioritising your fulfilment factors in your life.

Make hard work enjoyable

Identify a type of work that you do regularly that feels like drudgery. Now, name something you really enjoy that you could pair with this activity. Could you listen to your favourite music while replying to email?

Start to consistently pair the hard work with something that makes it more enjoyable and boosts your energy. If you do this often enough, you'll start to look forward to the activity that once felt like it was sucking the life out of you.

Set upper and lower bounds

Consider a big project you are currently working on. Working backwards from your deadline, set yourself an upper and lower bound for how much you need to accomplish each day to meet your deadline. Ideally, frame the upper and lower bounds as output as opposed to hours spent working on the task.

Make habits stick through emotion

Think about a new habit you want to create. Break down the new habit into its tiniest form – ideally something that takes thirty seconds or less. Link the new habit with something you currently do daily, such as going to bed at night. Finally, celebrate the behaviour. By linking the new behaviour with a positive emotion, it will start to become automatic.

Bring levity to hard work

The next time you have a big, hard task, contemplate how you can incorporate some humour or levity into the process. You might use visual humour by inserting a funny meme into the opening page of a report you are preparing. Or perhaps you might want to invite your project team to open all meetings with someone sharing a funny story or joke.

The Spark Joy folder

When you next feel a bit down or deflated, dig out some artefacts that spark joy for you. These might be photos, emails, feedback you've received or accomplishments (e.g. a certificate). Pop these artefacts into your digital or analogue Spark Joy Folder.

Moving forward, whenever you receive something that makes you feel happy, consider moving it to your Spark Joy folder.

Create gratitude triggers

Pick a daily behaviour along with one thing you want to be more consciously grateful for. Link this gratitude to your chosen behaviour. It might be as simple as thinking about what you are grateful for whenever you undertake the behaviour. Or you might incorporate it in a written form, such as writing a note to yourself that expresses the gratitude and saving a photo of it on the lock screen of your phone.

Let others go first

In the morning, set an intention for the day to let others go first. You might want to start slow and simply practise letting others go first in traffic. Once you get the hang of that, let others go first in a queue or through a door. And then apply it to interactions you have with people and let others go first in a meeting, for example, to give their point of view.

Buy time with money

Make a list of tasks that drain you of energy or time, or both. Pick the task that takes up the most time per week and investigate how much it would cost to pay someone else to do it. Try paying someone to do this task for four weeks. At the end of the experiment, reflect on how eliminating the task from your life has made you feel, how much time it has freed up, and whether it therefore feels like a good financial trade.

Remove recurring irritants

Make a list of recurring irritants in your life. These are tasks that you do regularly (daily or weekly) that frustrate you, annoy you or that you simply find boring. Remove the recurring irritants through: delegation; stopping the task; purchasing or creating a solution; or altering the activity so it's no longer irritating.

The 'I don't' rule

Create rules for activities that you don't want to do or that drain you of energy. Write them down, beginning with the words 'I don't'. When someone makes a request of you that breaks one of these rules, say 'no' by using the language 'I don't do X'.

Yes, but

The next time you have a request made on your time, pause before saying a blanket 'yes' or 'no'. Instead, look for a middle ground. Is there a way that you can help a bit, without overcommitting yourself? Frame your response as 'Yes, but . . .', outlining the limitations you are placing around your 'yes'. By doing this, you'll be able to be generous in your giving, but also uphold boundaries around your time.

The To-Don't list

Diarise a meeting with yourself once a month. Call it your 'To-Don't' meeting. Look back at the month that has just passed and ask yourself what de-energised or deflated you most during the month. Create a list of things you will not do the following month. Keep this list in eyesight of your desk to act as a constant reminder.

Time well spent

'Nothing is a waste of time if you use the experience wisely.'
                                                                – Auguste Rodin

Let me tell you a secret: I sometimes skip the conclusions in books. Conclusions aren't supposed to contain new content, so I figure I don't need to read them.

This conclusion doesn't break convention – I'm not about to tell you anything new. But I do want to finish with some wise words (okay, I won't oversell it – let's just say some 'words') to set you off into the world, armed with a ton of strategies, and ensure that the time you invested in reading this book was time well spent.

First, you might either be feeling excited or overwhelmed. If you are excited (presumably because there were lots of strategies you are keen to try out), then awesome! Go for it! But if you are feeling overwhelmed ('So many strategies! Where do I start?!'), just pick one. And it doesn't even have to be your favourite. Just pick one strategy that resonates with you and solves a problem you are experiencing. And commit to testing it out for a week. If it helps, keep doing it. If it doesn't, simply pick another one.

Someone smart once said that small changes eventually add up to huge results. And that's been my experience when I have experimented with literally every one of the strategies in this book.

I frequently use the Hemingway trick when finishing (or rather, not finishing) work for the day, which makes getting into flow the following morning close to effortless. King's trick of looking for odd-numbered groups of people has made events so much less scary for me. And I applied McKeown's upper and lower bounds while writing this book, a technique that helped immensely in writing 70,000 words in five months while also working full-time (and not losing my mind).

Now of course, there is another option: do nothing. And so many people make that choice – perhaps not deliberately – after reading a book about work and personal development. But in the case of a book about using your time wisely, let's face it: that would be a rookie mistake. You have just invested several hours of your life reading it, so let's make sure the time we have spent together leads to change.

Life doesn't have to be chaotic and 'crazy busy'. You don't have to be at the mercy of your calendar and inbox. And your phone shouldn't rule your life.

Remember, you have the same number of hours in the day as Beyoncé. Now you know how to use more of them wisely.

More resources

I finished writing this book at the end of 2021, and since then, I continue to interview amazing guests on *How I Work* who have talked about numerous other strategies that were unable to be included in this book. Search for 'How I Work' wherever you listen to your podcasts if you are hungry for more insight and expertise.

For all the downloadable tools and templates that accompany some of the techniques contained in this book, head to amantha.com/timewise to access them all for free.

References

How wisely are you using your time?
Research from the World Health Organization suggests we are working longer than ever before.
Frank Pega, Bálint, Náfrádi, Natalie C. Momena, Yuka Ujita, Kai N. Streichera, Annette M. Prüss-Üstün et al, 'Global, regional, and national burdens of ischemic heart disease and stroke attributable to exposure to long working hours for 194 countries, 2000–2016: A systematic analysis from the WHO/ILO Joint Estimates of the Work-related Burden of Disease and Injury', *Environment International*, Vol. 154, Sept 2021, accessed Jan 2022 at https://www.science direct.com/science/article/pii/S0160412021002208

A survey of nearly 3000 professionals in America
Rob Maurer, 'Remote Employees Are Working Longer Than Before', Society for Human Resource Management, 16 Dec 2020, accessed Jan 2022 at https://www.shrm.org/hr-today/news/hr-news/pages/remote-employees-are-working-longer-than-before.aspx

In research that spanned sixty-five countries, software giant Atlassian found that Australians' daily average working hours increased by 32 minutes per day.
'People are working longer hours during the pandemic', *The Economist*, 24 Nov 2020, accessed Jan 2022 at https://www.economist.com/graphic-detail/2020/11/24/people-are-working-longer-hours-during-the-pandemic

According to the Microsoft report, we are sending 45 per cent more chat messages per week
'The next great disruption is hybrid working – are we ready?', microsoft.com, 22 March 2022, accessed Jan 2021 at https://www.microsoft.com/en-us/worklab/work-trend-index/hybrid-work

PRIORITIES
Goal-setting is broken. This is how to fix it
people feel more motivated when using systems instead of goals.
L. Legault & M. Inzlicht, 'Self-determination, self-regulation, and the brain: Autonomy improves performance by enhancing neuroaffective responsiveness to self-regulation failure', *Journal of Personality and Social Psychology*, 105(1), 2012, pp 123–38, accessed Dec 2021 at https://psycnet.apa.org/record/2012-29188-001

Professors Gary Latham and Travor Brown actually investigated the effects of using systems instead of goals
Gary P. Latham & Travor C. Brown, 'The Effect of Learning vs. Outcome Goals on Self-Efficacy, Satisfaction and Performance in an MBA Program', *Applied Psychology: An International Review*, 55(4), Oct 2006, pp 606–23, accessed Dec 2021 at https://psycnet.apa.org/record/2006-20408-006

The critical step most people miss when making decisions
And psychologists have found that having unlimited time to make decisions can actually impair, not improve, how happy we are with the outcomes.
B. Schwartz, A. Ward, J. Monterosso, S. Lyubomirsky, K. White & D.R. Lehman, 'Maximizing versus satisficing: Happiness is a matter of choice,' *Journal of Personality and Social Psychology*, 83(5), 2002, pp 1178–97, accessed Dec 2021 at https://psycnet.apa.org/record/2002-18731-012

How asking the right questions will lead you to better decisions
apparently 44 per cent of lawyers would not recommend that young people pursue a career in law.
Sally Kane, 'The 10 Challengers About a Career As a Lawyer', thebalancecareers.com, 20 Nov 2019, accessed Jan 2022 at https://www.thebalancecareers.com/lawyer-career-drawbacks-2164594

Have you overcommitted yourself? You need the Iceberg Yes
Research led by Professor Justin Kruger from New York University's Stern School of Business found that people consistently underestimated how much time they need to complete a task.
J. Kruger & M. Evans, 'If you don't want to be late, enumerate: Unpacking reduces the planning fallacy', *Journal of Experimental Social Psychology*, 40(5), 2002, pp 586–98, accessed Dec 2021 at https://psycnet.apa.org/record/2004-17814-002

Likewise, a task people expected to take eight days would actually take fourteen
Roger Buehler & Dale Griffin, 'Planning, personality, and prediction: The role of future focus in optimistic time predictions', *Organizational Behavior and Human Decision Processes*, Volume 92, Issues 1–2, 2003, pp 80–90, accessed Dec 2021 at https://www.sciencedirect.com/science/article/pii/S074959780300089X

Never regret a decision again with this simple question
Sigmund Freud famously referred to this drive as the Pleasure Principle
William Needles, 'The Pleasure Principle, The Constancy Principle, and The Primary Autonomous Ego', 17(3), 1 July 1969, pp 808–25, accessed Jan 2022 at https://journals.sagepub.com/doi/abs/10.1177/000306516901700306

In a study published in the *Journal of Personality and Social Psychology*, participants had to evaluate various activities and plans
T. Eyal, N. Liberman, Y. Trope & E. Walther, 'The Pros and Cons of Temporally Near and Distant Action', *Journal of Personality and Social Psychology*, 86(6), 2004, pp 781–95, accessed Jan 2022 at https://psycnet.apa.org/record/2004-14304-001

How to decide which meetings you should attend
Research has consistently found that satisfaction with meetings predicts how satisfied we are with our jobs overall.
Hansen, Morton, *Great at Work: How Top Performers Do Less, Work Better and Achieve More*, Simon & Schuster, 2018

Get more done with a Might-Do list
In a study published in the *Personality and Social Psychology Bulletin*, people were asked to imagine visiting a supermarket with a friend
Y. Huang, L. Wang, & J. Shi, 'When do objects become more attractive? The individual and interactive effects of choice and ownership on object evaluation', *Personality and Social Psychology Bulletin*, 35(6), 2009, pp 713–22, accessed Dec 2021 at https://psycnet.apa.org/record/2009-08449-004

STRUCTURE
Why you need to let your chronotype shape your day
For example, research conducted in Iran with 210 health care workers
Fatemeh Amini, Seyed Mohammad Moosavi, Raheleh Rafaiee, Ali Asghar Nadi Ghara & Masoudeh Babakhanian, 'Chronotype patterns associated with job satisfaction of shift working healthcare providers', *Chronobiol Int*, 38(4), April 2021, pp 526–33, accessed Dec 2021 at https://pubmed.ncbi.nlm.nih.gov/33435743/

Build a satisfying highlight into every day
In one study led by Psychology Professor Gabriele Oettingen
G. Oettingen, M.K. Marquardt, & P.M. Gollwitzer, 'Mental contrasting turns positive feedback on creative potential into successful performance', *Journal of Experimental Social Psychology*, 48(5), 2012, pp 990–96, accessed Dec 2021 at https://psycnet.apa.org/record/2012-10398-001

Stop treating breaks as an afterthought
Research from the University of Colorado uncovered that there is an optimum length of time for breaks.
A. Bergouignan, K.T. Legget, N. De Jong et al, 'Effect of frequent interruptions of prolonged sitting on self-perceived levels of energy, mood, food cravings and cognitive function', *International Journal Behavioral Nutrition and Physical Activity*, 13, 113 (2016), accessed Dec 2021 at https://ijbnpa.biomedcentral.com/articles/10.1186/s12966-016-0437-z

In one study, after listening to a story, one group of people rested for 10 minutes
Michaela Dewar, Jessica Alber, Christopher Butler, Nelson Cowan & Sergio Della Sala, 'Brief Wakeful Resting Boosts New Memories Over the Long Term', *Psychological Science*, 23(9), pp 955–60, accessed Dec 2021 at https://journals.sagepub.com/doi/abs/10.1177/0956797612441220

How to stop mindless email checking
Research by Kostadin Kushlev and Elizabeth Dunn from the University of British Columbia found that people who checked their email three times per day were significantly less stressed than those who constantly dip in and out.
Kostadin Kushlev & Elizabeth W. Dunn, 'Checking email less frequently reduces stress', *Computers in Human Behavior*, Volume 43, Feb 2015, pp 220–28, accessed Dec 2021 at https://www.sciencedirect.com/science/article/abs/pii/S0747563214005810

Why you need to finish your day with the Hemingway Trick
Psychologist Bluma Zeigarnik ran a famous experiment in 1927
'The Zeigarnik Effect Explained', psychologistworld.com, accessed Jan 2022 at https://www.psychologistworld.com/memory/zeigarnik-effect-interruptions-memory

It's time to start a 'quitting-time' ritual
Psychologists have found that one of the biggest benefits of rituals such as this one is that they instil a sense of meaning in life.

Samantha J. Heintzelman & Laura A. King, 'Routines and Meaning in Life', *Personality and Social Psychology Bulletin*, 45(5), 18 Sept 2018, pp 688–99, accessed Dec 2021 at https://journals.sagepub.com/doi/full/10.1177/01461672 18795133

When it comes to the specific ritual of tidying up and putting things away, research published in *Psychological Science* suggests it's a highly beneficial ritual to adopt.
X. Li, L. Wei, & D. Soman, 'Sealing the emotions genie: The effects of physical enclosure on psychological closure', *Psychological Science*, 21(8), 2010, pp 1047–50, accessed Dec 2021 at https://psycnet.apa.org/record/2010 23598-001

EFFICIENCY
Why you need to go on a zombie hunt
Perhaps not surprisingly, research has found that people do not like to believe their past choices were misguided.
D.J. Sleesman, A.C. Lennard, G. McNamara & D.E. Conlon, 'Putting escalation of commitment in context: A multilevel review and analysis', *The Academy of Management Annals*, 12(1), 2018, pp 178–207, accessed Dec 2021 at https://psycnet.apa.org/record/2018-15084-007

A formula for more efficient meetings
In a study led by Professor Justin Kruger from New York University's Stern School of Business
J. Kruger, D. Wirtz, & D.T. Miller, 'Counterfactual Thinking and the First Instinct Fallacy', *Journal of Personality and Social Psychology*, 88(5), 2005, pp 725–35, accessed Dec 2021 at https://psycnet.apa.org/record/2005-04675-001

A simple strategy to reduce time wastage
Perhaps surprisingly, forcing ourselves to work and think fast improves our mood.
E. Pronin, E. Jacobs & D.M. Wegner, 'Psychological effects of thought acceleration', *Emotion*, 8(5), 2008, pp 597–612, accessed Dec 2021 at https://psycnet.apa.org/record/2008-13989-002

Some unusual research led by Echo Wen Wan
Echo Wen Wan & Brian Sternthal, 'Regulating the Effects of Depletion Through Monitoring', *Personality and Social Psychology Bulletin*, 34(1), 1 Jan 2008, pp 32–46, accessed Dec 2021 at https://journals.sagepub.com/doi/10.1177/0 146167207306756

Nudge your way to better behaviour
Research led by Paul Rozin from the University of Pennsylvania

P. Rozin, S. Scott, M. Dingley, J.K. Urbanek, H. Jiang & M. Kaltenbach, 'Nudge to Nobesity I: Minor Changes in Accessibility Decrease Food Intake', *Judgment and Decision Making*, 6 (4), 2011, pp 323–32, accessed Dec 2021 at https://repository.upenn.edu/cgi/viewcontent.cgi?article=1282&context=marketing_papers

How to stop forgetting what you read
One of Young's favourite studies into memory was conducted by Jeffrey Karpicke and Janell Blunt from Purdue University.

Jeffrey D. Karpicke & Janell R. Blunt, 'Retrieval Practice Produces More Learning than Elaborative Studying with Concept Mapping', *Science*, Vol 331, Issue 6018, 11 Feb 2011, pp 772–75, accessed Dec 2021 at https://www.science.org/doi/abs/10.1126/science.1199327

FOCUS
Focus: Get in Flow
Research collated by MediaKix suggests that around half of our phone time – nearly two hours – is spent on the top five social media platforms

'How much time do we spend on social media?', mediakik.com, accessed Dec 2021 at https://mediakix.com/blog/how-much-time-is-spent-on-social-media-lifetime/#gs.EQCxB7I

A review of studies published about mobile phone addiction

J. De-Sola Gutiérrez, F. Rodríguez de Fonseca & G. Rubio, 'Cell-Phone Addiction: A Review', *Frontiers in Psychiatry*, 7:175, 24 Oct 2016, accessed Jan 2022 at https://www.ncbi.nlm.nih.gov/pmc/articles/PMC5076301/

Get your phone off the table to boost happiness
Dunn and her colleagues set up an experiment to subtly manipulate how much people were using their phones during a social interaction

Ryan J. Dwyer, Kostadin Kushlev & Elizabeth W. Dunn, 'Smartphone use undermines enjoyment of face-to-face social interactions', *Journal of Experimental Social Psychology*, Volume 78, 2018, pp 233–39, accessed Dec 2021 at https://www.sciencedirect.com/science/article/abs/pii/S0022103117301737

How getting comfortable with discomfort will make you more productive

In one fascinating study, arachnophobic participants were asked to stand near a tarantula

Katharina Kircanski et al, 'Feelings into words: contributions of language to exposure therapy', *Psychological Science* vol. 23,10, 2012, pp 1086–91, accessed Dec 2021 at https://www.ncbi.nlm.nih.gov/pmc/articles/PMC4721564/

How to use music to get into flow

In one study published in the *Psychology of Sport and Exercise* journal, netball players were asked to select music

J. Pates, C.I. Karageorghis, R. Fryer & I. Maynard, 'Effects of asynchronous music on flow states and shooting performance among netball players', *Psychology of Sport and Exercise*, 4(4), 2003, pp 415–27, accessed Dec 2021 at https://psycnet.apa.org/record/2003-10506-008

An unconventional way to achieve creative flow

A study published in *Leadership Quarterly* examined how leaders could boost creativity within a team.

K.S. Jaussi & S.D. Dionne, 'Leading for creativity: The role of unconventional leader behavior', *The Leadership Quarterly*, 14(4-5), 2003, pp 475–98, accessed Dec 2021 at https://psycnet.apa.org/record/2003-09618-005

The real reason you're procrastinating

But after editing a piece on procrastination by Charlotte Lieberman, Herrera started to think differently.

Charlotte Lieberman, 'Why you procrastinate (it has nothing to do with self-control), *New York Times*, 25 March 2019, accessed Dec 2021 at https://www.nytimes.com/2019/03/25/smarter-living/why-you-procrastinate-it-has-nothing-to-do-with-self-control.html

Research led by Michael Wohl found that forgiving yourself for procrastinating leads to doing it less in the future.

Michael J.A. Wohl, Timothy A. Pychyl & Shannon H. Bennett, 'I forgive myself, now I can study: How self-forgiveness for procrastinating can reduce future procrastination', *Personality and Individual Differences*, 48, 2010, pp 803–8, accessed Jan 2022 at https://law.utexas.edu/wp-content/uploads/sites/25/Pretend-Paper.pdf

RFLECTION
Use self-doubt as a strength, not a weakness
Stanford University Psychologist Alia Crum

A.J Crum, P. Salovey & S. Achor, 'Rethinking stress: The role of mindsets in determining the stress response', *Journal of Personality and Social Psychology*, 104(4), 2013, pp 716–33, accessed Dec 2021 at https://psycnet.apa.org/record/2013-06053-001

Transform fear into excitement with this simple question
Research published in the *Journal of Positive Psychology* supports asking ourselves the question: What is the best thing that could happen?

Kathryn C. Adair, Lindsay A. Kennedy & J. Bryan Sexton, 'Three Good Tools: Positively reflecting backwards and forwards is associated with robust improvements in well-being across three distinct interventions', *The Journal of Positive Psychology*, 15:5, 2020, pp 613–22, accessed Dec 2021 at https://www.tandf online.com/doi/full/10.1080/17439760.2020.1789707

The ideal time to seek feedback
Scientists have investigated why this might be the case.

J.J. Dahling, & C.L. Ruppel, 'Learning goal orientation buffers the effects of negative normative feedback on test self-efficacy and reattempt interest', *Learning and Individual Differences*, 50, 2016, pp 296–301, accessed Dec 2021 at https://psycnet.apa.org/record/2016-40949-001

How to elicit feedback that's actually useful
When Young was writing *Ultralearning*, he spoke to Avraham Kluger

Avraham N. Kluger & Angelo DeNisi, 'The Effects of Feedback Interventions on Performance: A Historical Review, a Meta-Analysis, and a Preliminary Feedback Intervention Theory', *Psychological Bulletin*, Vol. 119, No. 2, 1996, pp 254–84, accessed Dec 2021 at https://mrbartonmaths.com/resourcesnew/8.%20Research/Marking%20and%20Feedback/The%20effects%20of%20feedback%20interventions.pdf

Remind yourself that you will die
Roman philosopher Seneca, one of the adherents to the Stoic movement, wrote about this in one of his essays, 'The Shortness of Life'

Seneca, *On the Shortness of Life: Life Is Long if You Know How to Use It*, Penguin Books, 2005

CONNECTION

Why you need a one-page operating manual

And he has created his own operating manual, accessible by anyone with an internet browser.

Darren's README page, about.gitlab.com, accessed Dec 2021 at https://about.gitlab.com/handbook/marketing/readmes/dmurph/

Sijbrandij has his own online operating page where he lists his major flaws.
Sijbrandij's CEO page, accessed Dec 2021 at https://about.gitlab.com/handbook/ceo/

Use an item of clothing to transform behaviour

In one unusual study lead by Amanda Shantz, employees at a fundraising call centre were given an information pack about their jobs.
A. Shantz & G.P. Latham, An exploratory field experiment of the effect of subconscious and conscious goals on employee performance. *Organizational Behavior and Human Decision Processes*, 109(1), 2009, pp 9–17, accessed Dec 2021 at https://psycnet.apa.org/record/2009-06254-003

How to be a better networker – without meeting new people

Research led by Daniel Levin from Rutgers Business School
Daniel Z. Levin, Jorge Walter & John Keith Murnighan, 'Dormant Ties: The Value of Reconnecting', *Organization Science*, 22(4), 2011, pp 923–39, accessed Dec 2021 at https://papers.ssrn.com/sol3/papers.cfm?abstract_id=1625543

While this might seem inconsequential, research has found that people tend to underestimate the effects of saying 'thank you' and giving someone a compliment.
Erica J. Boothby & Vanessa K. Bohn, 'Why a Simple Act of Kindness Is Not as Simple as It Seems: Underestimating the Positive Impact of Our Compliments on Others', *Personality and Social Psychology Bulletin*, 47 (5), 1 May 2021, pp 826–40, accessed Dec 2021 at https://journals.sagepub.com/doi/abs/10.1177/0146167220949003

How to avoid small talk when meeting new people

Cheri Levinson and her colleagues found that when people think about their unique experiences, stories, and qualities, they reported feeling less anxious during social gatherings.
Cheri A. Levinson, Julia K. Langer & Thomas L. Rodebaugh, 'Self-construal and social anxiety: Considering personality', *Personality and Individual Differences*, 51, 2011, pp 355–59, accessed Dec 2021 at http://www.cherilevinson.com/uploads/1/1/7/6/11768007/levinson_langer_rodebaugh.pdf

Make meeting new people at events less terrifying

Interestingly, if more introverted people act in an extroverted manner and undertake activities associated with extroversion

J.M. McNiel & W. Fleeson, 'The causal effects of extraversion on positive affect and neuroticism on negative affect: Manipulating state extraversion and state neuroticism in an experimental approach', *Journal of Research in Personality*, 40(5), 2006, pp 529–50, accessed Dec 2021 at https://psycnet.apa.org/record/2006-12442-005

ENERGY

It's 2 pm and you're flailing. You're in the classic 'post-lunch dip' phase of the day

Monk, Timothy, 'The Post-Lunch Dip in Performance', *Clinics in sports medicine*, 24(2), May 2005, accessed Dec 2021 at https://www.researchgate.net/publication/7848298_The_Post-Lunch_Dip_in_Performance

How a sticky note can help you be more resilient

In a rather unusual experiment, research led by Bruce Smith from the University of New Mexico

Bruce W. Smith, Erin M. Tooley, Erica Q. Montague, Amanda E. Robinson, Cynthia J. Cosper & Paul G. Mullins, 'The role of resilience and purpose in life in habituation to heat and cold pain', *The Journal of Pain*, 10(5). May 2009, pp 493–500, accessed Dec 2021 at https://pubmed.ncbi.nlm.nih.gov/19345153/

The optimal pace for hard work

Professor Maura Scott led research that demonstrated the impact of setting upper and lower bounds.

M.L. Scott & S.M. Nowlis, 'The effect of goal specificity on consumer goal reengagement', *Journal of Consumer Research*, 40(3), 2013, pp 444–59, accessed Dec 2021 at https://psycnet.apa.org/record/2013-32845-004

Why you need a Spark Joy folder

Our overemphasis on the negative has a name: Negativity Bias.

A. Vaish, T. Grossmann, & A. Woodward, 'Not all emotions are created equal: the negativity bias in social-emotional development', *Psychological Bulletin*, 134(3), 2008, pp 383–403. https://doi.org/10.1037/0033-2909.134.3.383, accessed Dec 2021 at https://www.ncbi.nlm.nih.gov/pmc/articles/PMC3652533/

How your computer password can make you more productive

Decades of research has shown that gratitude makes us feel good.

R.A. Emmons & M.E. McCullough, 'Counting blessings versus burdens: an experimental investigation of gratitude and subjective well-being in daily life', *Journal of Personality and Social Psychology*, 84(2), Feb 2003, pp 377–89, accessed Jan 2022 at https://pubmed.ncbi.nlm.nih.gov/12585811/#affiliation-1

J.J. Froh, W.J. Sefick & R.A Emmons, 'Counting blessings in early adolescents: an experimental study of gratitude and subjective well-being', *Journal of School Psychology*, 46(2), April 2008, pp 213–33, accessed Jan 2022 at https://pubmed.ncbi.nlm.nih.gov/19083358/#affiliation-1

people who kept a daily or weekly gratitude journal for ten weeks were significantly happier than those who wrote about neutral or negative life events.

R.A. Emmons & M.E. McCullough, ibid.

Other research found that teenagers who were asked to think about things they were grateful for reported significantly higher life satisfaction

J.J. Froh, W.J. Sefick & R.A. Emmons, ibid.

Why's it's worth considering buying more time

'We published a series of eight studies in one of the leading scientific journals demonstrating that people who use money to buy time are happier than those who don't.'

Ashley V. Whillans, Elizabeth W. Dunn, Paul Smeets, Rene Bekkers & Michael I. Norton, 'Buying time promotes happiness', *Proceedings of the National Academy of Sciences*, 114 (32), Aug 2017, pp 8523–27, accessed Dec 2021 at https://www.pnas.org/content/114/32/8523

How to remove recurring irritants from your life

It was because of a force called Tunnelling.

Anandi Mani, Sendhil Mullainathan, Eldar Shafir & Jiaying Zhao, 'Poverty Impedes Cognitive Function', *Science*, (341), Aug 2013, pp 976–80, accessed Dec 2021 at https://scholar.harvard.edu/files/sendhil/files/976.full_.pdf

The power of 'Yes, but'

Interestingly, research has shown that people tend to value and appreciate small acts of kindness more than anticipated.

Y. Zhang & N. Epley, 'Self-centered social exchange: Differential use of costs versus benefits in prosocial reciprocity', *Journal of Personality and Social Psychology*, 97(5), 2019, pp 796–810, accessed Dec 2021 at https://psycnet.apa.org/record/2009-19144-004

Acknowledgements

It was over a coffee at Babble in Prahran that this book was first given a chance at a life outside my head. I had been working on the concept for a few months when I was introduced to (my now agent) Cathy Baker from CMC Talent Management, who asked if I was working on any book ideas. I said 'yes'.

So first, Cathy, thank you for being so completely awesome and supportive, and for having an unwavering belief in me. I feel so fortunate to have you as a partner in crime (of the legal variety, obviously).

Cathy proceeded to matchmake my book idea with Isabelle Yates from Penguin Random House (PRH). Izzy, you have been the most passionate champion that a gal could ask for. I can't even begin to imagine how many ideas you get pitched every day and I still feel so ridiculously fortunate that you believed in what I wanted to do. I refer to you to my friends as my 'book captain', so thank you Captain Izzy for leading my book so enthusiastically through the world of PRH into this reader's hands. Thanks to your vision, ideas and feedback, you have been instrumental in making *Time Wise* infinitely more impactful.

Thank you to Clive Hebard at PRH who made the copyediting part of this process an absolute joy (when it could have been anything but). Clive, thank you for being oh-so-focused on the smallest details on every single page of the manuscript, and for not only injecting a billion improvements into my book but for also bringing humour to the process. (Who would have thought laughs could be had when talking about grammatical changes?)

Thank you to Braden Bird and Jemma Ferreira-Rowe from the PRH marketing and publicity team for helping to spread the word about *Time Wise* and being full of creative ideas on how to do so.

This book would not exist without the completely and utterly inspiring people I have had the absolute privilege of interviewing on *How I Work* over the last three years. You have all made what is work feel like anything but. A special shout-out to three of my heroes/guests – Adam Grant, Jake Knapp and Nir Eyal – who have been particularly generous with their time and support.

Since *How I Work* began in July 2018, my dad, Martin, has done the sound mix for every single episode. He went from being a retired engineer and computer programmer to learning how to be a sound engineer in the space of weeks (not to mention being an absolute guru on the best gear to use). Thank you for the hundreds (or is it now thousands?) of hours you have spent making me and my guests sound so much clearer and better, and for the love and care you put into every single episode. It has been such a joyous father-daughter project to work with you on.

In 2021, I expanded the *How I Work* team to include non-family members. Kellie Riordan, I was a fan of yours from afar and have now been lucky enough to have worked with you and the team at Deadset Studios for more than a year. Every podcaster needs a Kellie; you have made me an immeasurably better interviewer and have levelled up *How I Work* so, so much. A huge thank you to Jenna Koda for the hours and hours of research you put into the show every week, and to Liam Riordan for your savvy edits and assistance in making every episode far sharper.

Writing a book in five months while working full-time (although technically, we do a Four-day Week at Inventium) doesn't happen unless you have a superstar team supporting you. Thank you to the best CEO I could have dreamed of in Mish Le Poidevin and for steering the Inventium ship so well over the last three years (and especially during the craziness that was the last eighteen months).

And thank you to Charlotte Rush, Zoe Aitken, Nick Johnston, Georgia Luttick, Gabby Webb, Kez Hanstock, Sasha D'Arcy, Evelina Bereni and Hannah O'Connor for being the best team I could ever imagine working with. Working with you all means that every single workday guarantees new ideas to ponder, feedback to improve my thinking, a mutual cheer squad, and lots and lots of belly laughs.

Thank you to my mum, who is also a writer and psychologist, for inspiring me to become what she describes as a 'detective of the mind', as well as making me a far better writer through countless edits on so much of my work over the last three decades (including ones that made the very first draft of this manuscript far better). More importantly, thank you for being my rock and for the unconditional love I always know is there waiting for me.

As an only child, I have always said that my friends are the family I chose. And I have made some bloody good choices over the years. A special thank you to Monique, Trudi, Simon (Mrocki), Simon (Moss), Steph, Tash, Sarah, Sean, Jase, Mia and Andrew for bringing much laughter, wisdom and damn good company to my life, especially during the Melbourne lockdowns and other challenges as I was writing this book.

I dedicated this book to my daughter Frankie (who was rather excited about that decision). And while she probably won't read it (although I'm tempted to prescribe it to her as bedtime reading), I want to thank her for inspiring me every day with her curiosity for the world.

About the author

Dr Amantha Imber is an organisational psychologist and founder of behavioural science consultancy Inventium. Amantha is also the co-creator of the *Australian Financial Review*'s Most Innovative Companies list and the AFR BOSS Best Places to Work list. Amantha has helped companies such as Google, Apple, Disney, Lego, Atlassian, Commonwealth Bank and many others reinvent the way they approach their work.

In 2019, Amantha was named as one of the *Australian Financial Review*'s 100 Women of Influence.

In 2021, she won the *Thinkers50* Innovation Award (described by the *Financial Times* as the 'Oscars for Management Thinking'), which recognises the thinker who has contributed the most to the understanding of innovation globally over the last two years. Amantha was the first Australian to win this award.

Amantha is also the host of the number one ranking business podcast *How I Work*, which has had more than 3 million downloads, where she interviews some of the world's most successful people about their habits, strategies and rituals.

Amantha's thoughts have appeared in *Harvard Business Review*, *Forbes*, *Entrepreneur* and *Fast Company*, and she is the author of two bestselling books: *The Creativity Formula* and *The Innovation Formula*.

amantha.com
inventium.com.au
Amantha Imber
@amantha
@amanthai